STEEL
WIRE
JEWELRY

STEEL WIRE JEWELRY

Stylish Designs · Simple Techniques
Artful Inspiration

BRENDA SCHWEDER

LARK CRAFTS

An Imprint of Sterling Publishing Co., Inc.
New York

WWW.LARKCRAFTS.COM

Editor
Marthe Le Van

Assistant Editor
Gavin R. Young

Editorial Assistance
Abby Haffelt

Art Director
Kristi Pfeffer

Junior Designer
Carol Morse Barnao

Project Photography
Steve Mann
blackboxphoto.info

Instructional Photography
Tom Fritz
tomfritz.com

Illustrations
Brenda Schweder

Cover Designer
John Barnett

Library of Congress Cataloging-in-Publication Data

Schweder, Brenda.
  Steel wire jewelry : stylish designs, simple techniques, artful inspiration / Brenda Schweder. -- 1st ed.
    p. cm.
  Includes index.
  ISBN 978-1-60059-538-7 (pb-trade pbk. : alk. paper)
  1. Jewelry making. 2. Wire craft. I. Title.
  TT212.S383 2011
  739.27--dc22
                                      2010003895

10 9 8 7 6 5 4 3 2 1

First Edition
Published by Lark Crafts, An Imprint of
Sterling Publishing Co., Inc.
387 Park Avenue South, New York, NY 10016

Text © 2011, Brenda Schweder

Photography © 2011, Lark Crafts, An Imprint of Sterling Publishing Co., Inc., unless otherwise specified

Illustrations © 2011, Lark Crafts, An Imprint of Sterling Publishing Co., Inc.

Distributed in Canada by Sterling Publishing,
c/o Canadian Manda Group, 165 Dufferin Street
Toronto, Ontario, Canada M6K 3H6

Distributed in the United Kingdom by GMC Distribution Services,
Castle Place, 166 High Street, Lewes, East Sussex, England BN7 1XU

Distributed in Australia by Capricorn Link (Australia) Pty Ltd.,
P.O. Box 704, Windsor, NSW 2756 Australia

If you have questions or comments about this book, please contact:
Lark Crafts
67 Broadway
Asheville, NC 28801
828-253-0467

Manufactured in China

ISBN 13: 978-1-60059-538-7

For information about custom editions, special sales, and premium and corporate purchases, please contact the Sterling Special Sales Department at 800-805-5489 or specialsales@sterlingpub.com.

For information about desk and examination copies available to college and university professors, requests must be submitted to academic@larkbooks.com. Our complete policy can be found at www.larkcrafts.com.

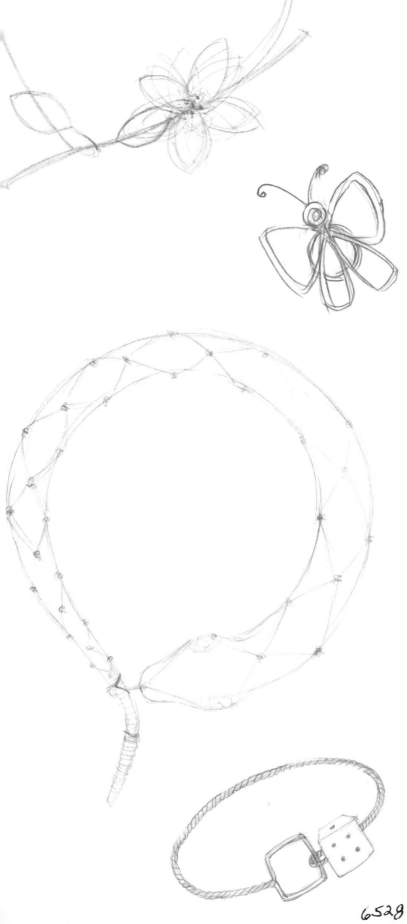

6528

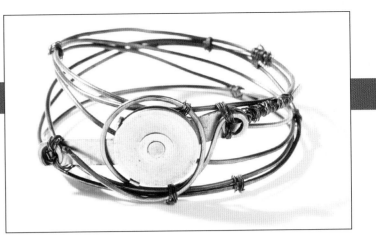

foreword
STEELING BEAUTY

In the search for interesting materials with which to create, the greatest surprises can come from the most unexpected quarters.

In the frenzied, ecstatic first months of my immersion into the world of jewelry and sculpture made with found objects, I found myself pulled back time and again to the local hardware store. That environment triggered more creative energy in me than the most complete art supply store on the planet ever did. It was on one of those hardware hikes that I happened upon a roll of grey, slightly rusty rebar wire nestled forlornly between cinder blocks. It looked like it had been there forever, like the store was built around it. I marveled at the weight of this coil as I lifted it from its dusty perch, and with hands already darkening, took it to the counter. Three measly dollars lighter, I hauled it home.

Although I was still years away from any organized instruction in metalworking, I was smitten immediately with this annealed, or heat-softened, steel: the buttery give to a tweak of the hand, combined with just enough resistance to remind you that you weren't in Copperland any more. There was the tremendous latitude of the wire—it could be bent and unbent repeatedly while working it, without fear of breakage. Then, of course, there was the color—ranging from coal black to a chrome gleam.

Simply put: love.

Yet, like any lasting relationship, it has given up its secrets slowly. More than two decades on from that sweet discovery, I find I'm still learning daily about this remarkable material. Many silversmithing techniques are easily applied to steel wire, albeit with a tad more grunt and a few alterations. But it's absolutely its own animal, as different from silver and gold in look and behavior as ebony from pine.

For all its many charms, steel wire remains even today an outsider in the jewelry world, which only increases its appeal for me. But more and more people are discovering the unique properties that only it possesses. Having taught thousands of people about this stuff over the years seems at last to be manifesting in a wider acceptance of the material, if this lovely and fun book by Brenda Schweder is any indication.

Now get in there and get your hands (gloriously) dirty.

Keith Lo Bue
www.lobue-art.com

8

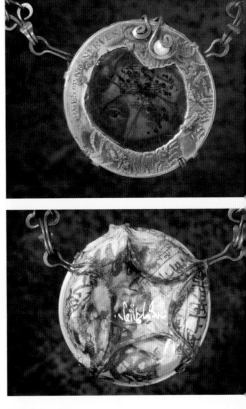

Keith Lo Bue
NERVES OR NO NERVES?, 2004
Jelly mold, brass, waxed linen thread, costume pearl, 17th century kozo paper, color lithograph, 1920s fabric and tassels, paper, steel, leather, mica, soil
Photos by artist

Left: **Keith Lo Bue**
Two Sides of History, 2009
Antique animal trap, keyholes, glass, drawer pull, optometrist's lens, steel eye, bolt, brass ring, upholstery tacks, thimble, seaweed root, pearl, photograph, nickel silver, antique ear nuts, steel
Photo by artist

introduction

THE PROVERBIAL COIL OF WIRE

I've started this artist's note in my head probably a hundred times over. The process went sort of like a Dr. Seuss book.

I thought in a box,

sat on some rocks,

hung from a tree,

(nearly stung by a bee).

I tried on a bike,

walked a long hike,

mulled on the way

to a play,

one day . . .

by the way.

Robert Ebendorf
Around The Team, 2009
7.6 cm in diameter
Steel wire, pearls, silver, paper, mixed media
Photo by artist

But the harder I tried, the harder it became. Explaining what in the world is so compelling about a 3-pound coil of steel wire actually left me speechless. And wordless. And who-would-ever-believe-this?

In the raw, it's dirty, it's heavy, and it's most certainly lackluster. It's the proverbial lump of clay (but not clay at all).

I guess it's just that—that diamond-in-the-rough quality—that's so gripping. Maybe that's what artists who throw clay on a wheel or sculpt blocks of marble

or turn intricate wooden urns on a lathe feel— that sense of discovery of the treasure beneath, that unearthing of a yet-to-be-found cache. It's a heart-fluttering thing for those of us who need to work with our hands and a super-rush for the adventurer in us.

I know that's what leads me to create so much of my work. The thrill of taking something so ordinary, so dime-a-dozen, and transforming it (voila!) into something special and uncommon stirs my heart. (It also causes that really dumb-looking smile to creep across my face in utter, undying contentment.)

Brenda Schweder
Safest Songbird, 2008
10.2 x 11.4 x 3.2 cm
Enamel, copper, steel, crystal
Photo by Deone Jahnke

Brenda Schweder
Bale Ring, 2009
3.8 x 2.5 x 3.2 cm
Steel, pyrite
Photo by Deone Jahnke

Yes, just like a lot of you, I have a lovely studio with more lovely beads than I care to admit, but it's the treasure trove of my found objects—that rusty bottle cap I embarrassed myself by picking up on the sidewalk; that goofy already-dead beetle Deb's kids saved for me; that vintage erector set Luci picked up as a "just-because" gift at the flea market—that moves me like nothing else.

So I've decided that within the ordinary, lies the profound. You almost have to try it yourself to *get* the thrill-of-the-pound beat, beat, beating in your soul. Sometimes it's just that simple. As simple (and insightful) as Dr. Seuss!

Brenda Schweder

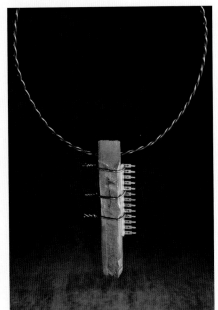

Brenda Schweder
Scrapyard No.1, 2009
53.3 x 10.2 cm
Bronze, steel, found electronic component
Photo by Deone Jahnke

basics

There's a "new guy" in Jewelry Town, and he's amazing!

Have you met him?

He's Steel Wire.

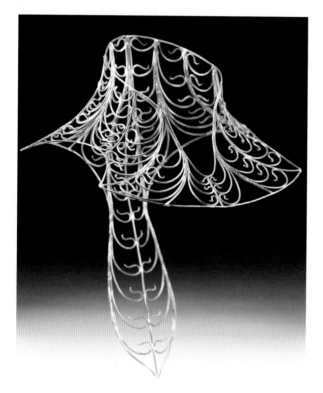

Natasha Seedorf
Tracery II, 2007
35.5 x 30.5 x 23 cm
Steel wire; formed, soldered, wire brushed
Photo by artist

Actually, he's lived here all along, but we're just getting to know Steel in a different way. We've grown, and we're seeing him with different eyes. He's definitely catching our attention now that we're "so inclined."

"Now come on," you ask yourself, "I thought steel wire was just used in construction—as reinforcement for giant skyscrapers, cement walls, and massive bridges." Well, you're right . . . and you're wrong. In a smaller gauge than the girders and textured rod you've seen in city demo sites, steel wire is used to construct super jewelry, too.

This type of wire has a bit of glamour to it. It's urban and edgy with ample allure. It's more muscular than other jewelry wires, such as silver and gold. It's unassuming in its origin, but makes a huge aesthetic impact. Its look is casual and robust and can mimic the heartiness of oxidized sterling silver. You may not find Steel on the fashion runway just yet, but now is definitely the time for his big break.

Steel wire has some very attractive character traits.

Workability

Steel wire is sold in a dead soft state. It work hardens and stays workable for a lot longer than other jewelry wires, which become brittle and snap with too much finessing.

Ji Eun Lee
Dependence, 2009
8.9 x 5.1 x 5.1 cm
Steel wire, cement,
paint; soldered
Photo by artist

Marlene True
St. Elsie, 2008
7.5 x 3.8 x 3.8 cm
Steel wire, tin, silver, enamel paint;
formed, forged, soldered, die cut
Photo by Ralph Gabriner

Accessibility

You can find steel wire at your local hardware store or home improvement center.

Affordability

Steel wire's got a bargain-basement price—and don't we frugal-McDoogals *love* that?

You can't work with steel wire if you're afraid of making a mess. Getting dirty is just part of the package when designing with this hot new jewelry material. Be ready to roll up your sleeves and keep a tub of waterless hand cleanser on your worktable. The wire's carbon finish shows no mercy. Expect a lot of grime on your hands, some on your clothes, and a smidge of a smudge on your nose because of that itch you just had to scratch.

Steel Wire Jewelry will make the necessary introductions between you and your new love interest. You'll find out all about Steel's profile info, his likes and loathes. You'll learn about his twists and turns—how he reinvents himself and how he's different from all the other (wire metal) guys. Charles Lewton-Brain even gets involved in this little tryst with a history that goes way back.

You will find out how to work with steel to create many fabulous jewelry designs—from getting to know each other with some simple bends and twists, to combining different gauges, to chain making and captures (prongs, bails, and bezels). There's also a segment on Calder-inspired works and a chapter on how well this "guy" mixes with others (gemstones, tin, linen). He's a dream to introduce to your mother('s lace). There's even a gallery of fabulous works by other steel wire artists—he's a popular guy!

Yep, Steel's the tall, dark, and handsome type. He's strong but very approachable, moldable, and friendly (work friendly, that is!). Are you ready for a new relationship? Look out! This guy will sweep you off your feet! (Swooooon... !)

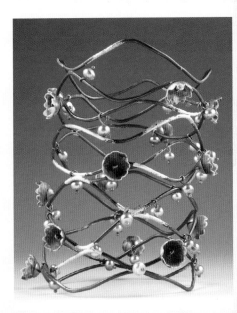

Kathryn Osgood
Bracelet with Roses, 2007
12 x 7.5 x 7.5 cm
Steel wire, fine silver, sterling silver,
gold leaf, enamel; soldered
Photo by artist

STEEL: ORIGINS & PROPERTIES

Iron has been used in a plethora of applications since the Iron Age. (Isn't it great to write about something that sports its own Age?) Iron and steel, though often used interchangeably, are not the same stuff. Iron is a pure element with its own place on the periodic table. Steel is a metal alloy, a mixture of iron and up to 2 percent carbon. Different alloy recipes produce different types of steel. You're sure to know a few: stainless, surgical stainless, tool, and mild. Steel was used to a great extent until the invention of a funky little substance called plastic. Remember when cars and toasters, and even hair doo-dads, were made exclusively of steel?

A Little History

A funny thing happened on the way to the refinery— steel's historic timeline has encountered a few blips on the radar screen dating from the time of its discovery until its ubiquitous presence in today's world. Iron, despite having its own place on the periodic table, isn't abundantly found in its pure form except for a few meteors and some small deposits worldwide. For that reason, other metals like gold, silver, bronze, and copper were in use some 5,000 years before iron came on the scene (explaining why the Iron Age follows those of stone and bronze). Iron is referred to in the Bible (Aaron's sacred robes), has adorned a Pharaoh (as part of an ancient Egyptian necklace), and has protected brave Saracen and Turkish knights (as chain armor during the Crusades). These applications were all accomplished by cold means—hammering and forging.

Due to iron's hardness and high melting point (approximately 2700°F/1482°C), the process of refining iron had to wait until the mid-19th century, when Sir Henry Bessemer discovered the open hearth process, which enabled furnaces to reach the temperatures necessary to work the metal hot.

Fashion and industry have played big parts in steel wire's history; and by big, I mean big-skirted. Between 1860 and 1870, crinoline wire was the main structure under trendy hoop skirts—about 1,500 net tons of wire were used for these each year. Corsets also did their duty to prop up the steel wire business, as another 13,600 metric tons per year were consumed in their heyday. Not to be outdone, the hairpin also did its thing beginning in 1916. The mid- to late 1800s also saw the invention of barbed wire, the telegraph and telephone, high-sulfur screw stock, coiled wire springs, woven-wire fence, the first American-made wire-nail machine, and the first steel-wire nails.

You get the picture. Steel wire is all around us, and that's just wire. Steel is one of the most commonly used materials in the world. We live and work in steel (houses and high-rises), move from place to place in steel (cars, boats, trains, and airplanes), sit on steel (upholstery springs), keep bugs out (window and door screening), and chickens in (chicken wire) with steel, and eat with steel ("silver" ware).

Ralph Wiley
Untitled, 2007
5.4 x 2 x 0.5 cm
Steel wire found object,
24-karat gold plate
Photo by artist

Coils of steel wire in various gauges

How It's Made

Steel wire is economical to produce, readily available, and easy to use. Most steel products are first formed into steel rod directly from iron ore. The rods are then *drawn* (pushed and pulled) through successively smaller tapered holes in a *drawplate* (made of a harder metal) until the desired diameter (or *gauge*) is reached.

How It's Measured

A little knowledge goes a long way in helping you understand how to use steel wire. A wire's gauge indicates its thickness; the higher the number of the gauge, the thinner the wire. While it's important to note that all wire is measured and sold in gauges, *ferrous* wire (wire containing iron) and *nonferrous* wire (all other wire types) are measured by different standards.

Yifat Bareket
bracelet, 2005
10 x 10 x 6.5 cm
Pearls, jasper, Swarovski crystal,
garnet, gold, silver, steel wire;
cast, set, welded, knitted
Photo by artist

STEEL WIRE GAUGE

GAUGE	INCHES	MILLIMETERS
28	0.0162	0.411
24	0.0230	0.584
20	0.0348	0.89
19	0.0410	1.04
18	0.0475	1.22
16	0.0625	1.57
12	0.1055	2.69

Historically, wire manufacturers in the United States each set their own gauges for steel wire stock. This changed around 1830, when the Bureau of Standards asked the industry to standardize and adopt one set of designations. First known as the Washburn & Moen system, the current standard is known as the United States Steel Wire Gauge (USSWG), or the Steel Wire Gauge (SWG) system. (The nonferrous wire industry has set its own gauge system, called the Brown & Sharpe or American Wire Gauge.)

Measuring wire in gauges is gradually falling from favor. Users prefer straightforward and consistent measuring standards for both ferrous and nonferrous wire. Eventually both types of wire will be measured in absolute units (thousandths of an inch and/or in millimeters). For now, however, use the table above to translate.

Why It's Dirty

Steel, like other wires, is most malleable in a dead soft state. (Any movement of the wire, such as bending with pliers or forging with a hammer, hardens it. This development is called work hardening.) To achieve optimum malleability, manufacturers coil the steel wire, anneal it to a certain temperature, and then slowly cool it. (Cooling the steel too quickly renders the material brittle and unusable.) Because the wire is exposed to air while at elevated temperatures, a scaly oxide forms on its surface, and that oxide transfers to hands, clothes, work surfaces, anything it touches.

About Its Strength & Ductility

The mechanical characteristics of steel—its hardness, stiffness, ductility, and tensile strength, for example—are affected by its chemical composition (percent of any added alloy material) as well as how it's manipulated in the factory. Steel wire's *ductility*—its ability to deform *plastically* without breaking—is much greater and therefore more tolerant of being worked than are other metals.

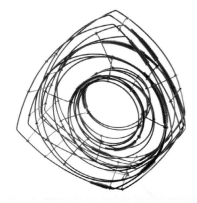

Donna D'Aquino
Wire Bracelet #88, 2004
17.8 x 17.8 x 6.4 cm
Steel wire
Photo by Ralph Gabriner

When It's Inclined to Corrode (Rust)

The most prevalent corrosion and worst surface contaminant to occur on steel is rust. Rust results when oxygen and water act on steel's surface; the result is a crusty reddish-brown coating. Rust prevents adhesion of any protective sealant and, if not removed but only covered, leads to increased corrosion and eventually to the metal's failure. In dry climates, brushing with a wire brush is sufficient to clean rust from the wire's surface.

Steel & the Environment

Steel was "green" long before recycling was cool! It's one of the most recycled materials in the world and *the* most recycled material in the United States. In 2007, over 60 million metric tons were reclaimed and refashioned into cars, buildings, and a million other things we use each day.

So here's to steel wire and its wondrous strength and adaptability! Join me in the following pages to see how this remarkable material also lends itself beautifully to creating unique, artistic jewelry.

Sara Sally LaGrand
Ripe, 2009
7.6 x 55.9 cm
Wire, glass; wrapped, lampworked
Photo by artist

Jill L. Erickson
Quartz Drop Necklace, 2009
45 x 2 cm
Steel wire, quartz; forged
Photo by Deone Jahnke

IRON & STEEL JEWELRY

A GLOBAL HISTORY

When Brenda Schweder asked me to add my thoughts on iron and steel jewelry, I was pleased by the opportunity. Pure iron is one of the least allergenic of all metals. Working with iron and steel connects you deeply to the history of jewelry making and to the meanings and magic that people ascribe to this special metal.

Humans have decorated themselves since they first gained consciousness. When iron was discovered, it clearly was used as jewelry. Iron, like fiber, does not always survive through time, so many historical examples are missing. But there are numerous instances of ancient iron jewelry from the Middle East, China, North Africa, and India.

Ancient Greece & Rome

The Spartans and other Greeks regularly wore iron rings as a symbol of strength. Early betrothal (engagement) rings in Rome were iron, sometimes set with *adamants* or diamond crystals. Roman senators and officials wore iron rings, only donning gold rings while representing Rome overseas or for major events. Most ordinary citizens weren't permitted to wear gold, only iron. Later in Roman life, citizens wore gold and silver, while wearing iron became an outward sign of enslavement.

Africa & The Middle East

Iron jewelry is common across many African cultures. Examples dating from 1000 BC were uncovered at the temple of Hathor in Egypt. In Africa and elsewhere, the choice of iron is not just about cost or easy access—it is considered protective. Iron jewelry is a talisman, worn to keep one safe, in good health, and free from harm of all kinds. African iron jewelry sometimes has attachments or pockets to hold medicine and to increase the strength of its effectiveness. Arabians used iron charms inscribed with words, and kept extensive lists of what properties these ornaments possessed.

Europe & America

Iron was used universally as a charm in European cultures, where it was believed to protect against evil spirits, lend physical strength, draw out illnesses and heal, and even produce invisibility. In Ireland, iron would be placed into a baby's bed to prevent it being stolen by the fairies. "Of all substances the little people feared iron most." (*Transactions*, Volume 21, page 268, Gaelic Society of Inverness, 1899.) Even today, it is tradition for Scottish fishermen to touch iron as a talisman against evil and the devil. After a death, iron was stuck into meat, cheese, and whiskey "to prevent death entering them." (*Encyclopaedia of Superstitions: A History of Superstition*, M. Radford and E. Radford, page 99, 2006.)

In the early nineteenth century, Berlin cast iron jewelry was developed. By 1815, it became a patriotic act to give up your gold and silver jewelry to fund a revolution against Napoleon. When you donated, you received iron brooches and rings in exchange for your precious metals. This patriotic jewelry became fashionable, and

Charles Lewton-Brain
Ironclad Ring, 2009
2.4 x 1 cm
Iron; forged
Photo by artist

in Victorian times this and other iron jewelry was commonly worn. During the first World War, more than 10,000 German New Yorkers gave their gold rings in exchange for iron rings to fund widows and orphans in Germany. I have seen English black iron wedding rings that widows received when their husbands were killed. They had *Pro Patria Mori* (Died for His Country) engraved on them.

Working in steel wire gives you a direct link with Alexander Calder, the artist who invented the mobile (hanging sculpture) and made hundreds of interactive, mechanical circus figures from steel wire. In the 1940s and 1950s, Calder created innovative hammered wire jewelry from steel, brass, and silver.

Today, steel jewelry is used mostly for fashion or status. Sikh men must wear a steel bracelet called a Kara, traditionally made of *loh*, iron or mild steel. Graduating engineers in Canada have an induction ritual after which they wear a steel ring on their little finger. This is a reminder of their responsibility for lives and a symbol of pride and humility.

Soft, ductile, full of meaning and history, steel wire is a wonderful material for making jewelry. Brenda Schweder is to be congratulated for her excellent work in bringing this approach to you.

Charles Lewton-Brain

Richard Salley
Untitled, 2006
12 x 14 cm
Steel wire, steel washer, river stone, upholstery tack; hammered, cold connected
Photo by artist

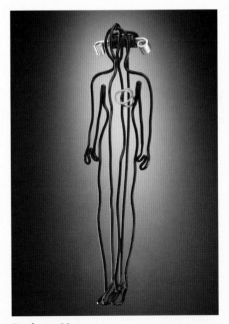

Barbara Mann
IRON WOMAN with Golden Heart and Sterling Attributes (Fibula), 2009
11 x 3 x 2 cm
Steel wire, 14-karat gold, sterling silver; forged, formed, soldered
Photo by Walker Montgomery

BASIC TOOLS & TECHNIQUES

Working with steel wire—everything from moving and forming to texturing, cleaning, and finishing—can be accomplished with your fingers and a few simple tools. In this section, I'll cover the techniques, tools, and supplies you'll need to accomplish any of these simple manipulations.

Keep the tools you use for working with steel separate from those you might use for working on more costly metals such as sterling silver or gold. Steel is a hard-working wire that's a little rough around the edges and a little dirty coming home, so you'll want to save your finer tools from gouges, mars, and rust.

A few specific tools are essential, some can be improvised, and some are not really tools at all but are just plain fun to have around. (In the way I like to sculpt with wire, many unconventional tools work for me. I'm kind of a clearance-aisle gal!) When working with steel wire, there's no significant advantage to having a lovely set of precision tools. (The tools you'll see in this chapter are the ones I used to make all the projects in this book.) But don't trade price for efficiency and productivity. If the tool doesn't do the job the way you want it to, you may as well discard it (or use it in one of your other found-object projects like I do!)

Use Cutters to Cut

I use a hefty flush cutter (photo A) for most of my cutting work. This is particularly important because steel wire is hard! Steel will mar the blades of fine-wire cutters. (Goodness, don't use your high-end cutters on steel!) The flush cutter can get into tighter spaces, like cutting that last little nibblet from the end of a wire wrap. It's also a hand-saver. It's up to the job of cutting this hard stuff. You want your cutter to work for you and not place undue stress on your mitts.

Use a memory-wire cutter (photo B) only for thin gauges of wire. This tool has scissor-like blades that aren't especially useful for cutting heavier gauges or for getting into tight areas. If you want to hold off investing in a good pair of flush cutters, memory-wire cutters will work in a pinch. A general-purpose, hardware-store wire cutter (photo C) and scissor shear (photo D) are also good for all-around work.

Use Mallets to Straighten

Mallets—either rawhide or plastic—move metal wire without hardening it. Use a mallet to straighten kinks, undo off-the-roll marks, and (especially) erase mistakes.

Remember, steel wire's number-one gift is extending playtime. Sometimes you just don't want to go back to the beginning and now you don't have to! Much of the time, you can simply stop pounding, straighten the wire with a mallet, and remake a step or two.

Peter Hoogeboom
Healing Heart, 1992
5 x 4 x 2.5 cm
Steel wire, broken glass; tin soldered
Photo by artist

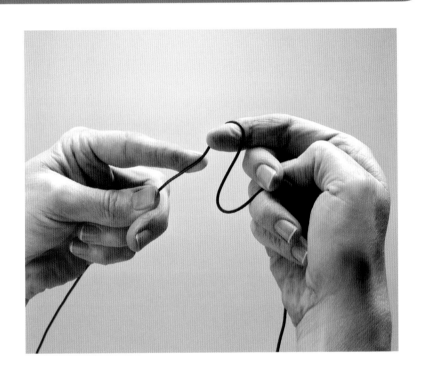

Debbi Simon
Flowering Aster, 2009
11.4 x 11.4 cm
Steel wire, resin inlay; formed
Photo by artist

Use Hands to Manipulate or Form

Creating with steel wire harkens to the industrial age in more than one way. When working with your hands, be prepared to get them dirty. If you're a bit of a neat-freak, keep waterless hand cleaner or wipes nearby. If you don't emerge from the workshop with filthy hands and a black smudge somewhere on your face, you need to go back and dig in a little more! Your hands are fundamental tools—don't be afraid to use them. Get right in there and feel your work come to life!

Rebecca A. McLaughlin Neigher
Meandering, 2008
42 x 1.8 cm
Steel wire, Lucite, sterling silver; formed, forged
Photo by artist

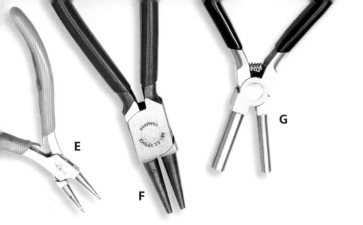

Use Pliers & Mandrels to Curve

When you want to form a structured curve or circle, use anything that will give you the size and shape you need. Work with any tubular object that can stand up to the job and not cave in under pressure. Hard plastics or metals—even some glass objects—are best.

Round-nose pliers (photos E and F) are the cat's meow for smaller projects. Their conical jaws give you a plethora of small areas to bend around, depending on where you place your wire. And forming pliers (photo G) give you a nice next-size-up to form around. I even make small batches of jump rings on these, since their jaws are of consistent size. Mandrels are great for forming any size circumference as well as for making jump rings by the dozen. Formal jewelry making mandrels are fab, but it's also a lot of fun to roam the house or studio looking for just the right knitting needle, marker, can, or bottle to form that perfect curved shape (photo H).

No matter the type of mandrel used, always bend the wire at the point of contact. Use your thumb to push the wire against the tool (photo 1) instead of holding the wire farther from the action and drawing it against the tool, as shown in photo 2. The latter causes gaps above the form; you may as well have not used a tool in the first place since you haven't followed the tool's shape.

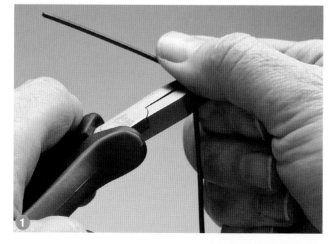

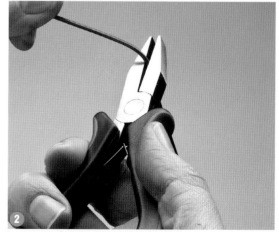

Use Flat-Nose Pliers to Form Angles

The jaws of flat-nose pliers have flat and flush interior surfaces (photo I).
To get a nice crisp bend in your wire, place the jaw's edge of flat-nose
pliers just beside the intended fold line, and bend the wire at the
point of contact. If the angle you're working to achieve is greater than
a right angle, start the bend with this method but pick up a second
tool to hold the wire very close to the fold and continue to bend to
the desired angle (photo 3).

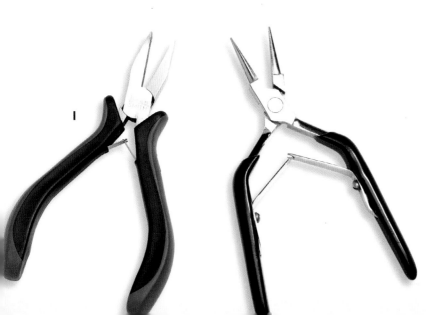

I

J

If you're trying to bend more than one piece of wire at the same point simultaneously, it's handy to use a vise. Position the piece to be bent in the vise so that the fold line is just above the edge of the jaws. Tighten the vise, and as shown in photo 4, use your fingers (covered here by protective gloves) or a mallet to bend the wire against the inner top edge of the vise.

Use Bent-Nose Pliers or a Vise to Hold

Use bent-nose pliers (photo J) and/or a vise as a "third hand" to stabilize the wire while you work with it. Bent-nose pliers allow you to firmly grip a piece in a fraction of the space your fingers would take up, and most of the tool is out of the way. Reminder: For particularly particular projects, cover the jaws of a vise with bits of leather, rubber, or foam to protect the wire from being marred.

Use a Hammer & Bench Block to Flatten, Forge & Texture

Really, any old hammer will do. I use a regular claw hammer (photo K) for most of my hardening and forging and a ball-peen hammer (photo L) to create a bit of "Ye-Olde-Blacksmith's" dappled texture. (Resist using any specialized tools that are designed for finer metals. Residual oxides can rust tools or worse, your finer metal work.)

4

You'll do most of your flattening, forging, and texturing work on top of a steel bench block (photo M). This strong, level surface provides ample support.

Keep in mind that pounding overlapping steel wires—especially in a small area—will break them. Of course, you may want to try a controlled version of this "no no" to achieve the cool hammered look of the String Art Earrings on page 41.

K   L   M   N   O

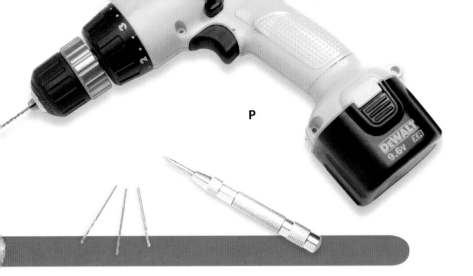

P

Use a Drill to Twist Wire

The community college near my home has a neat-o hand tool to twist wire, but there's no need to invest in one if you already have a power drill (photo P) or power screwdriver in the house. Simply fold a length of wire in half, making sure it is longer than needed. Secure one end of the folded wire in the drill chuck and tighten. Secure the other end in a vise. Stand back so that the wire is taut, and slowly pull the drill trigger. Twist the wire to the desired tension. (Twist on a Twist Bracelet, on page 50, walks you through the process in further detail.)

Use Files to Smooth Burrs & Rough Ends

Filing wire probably isn't anyone's idea of how to spend a grand afternoon but it's a necessity, especially for wearables. It's a good thing filing doesn't take long, especially the way I do it. My signature look is loose and lax—I file just enough to keep my fingers from getting scratched during a skin-brush test. I use un-fancy, medium-sized files (photo O) and small needle file sets (photo N)—whatever I can get away with to accomplish the task at hand.

Use Steel Wool, Wire Brushes & Your Hands to Clean

Now you need a way to get rid of the soot-like oxide on the wire's surface (a present from the wire manufacturer). Here are a few tricks you can pull out of your cleaning bag. You'll soon get to know what cleaning method works best for which type of project.

• Fine steel wool is my top pick. It glides over every surface and fits in every little cranny.

• Wire brushes are a close second because they're easy to hold. I use a suede brush from a local shoe repair shop. Brass bristles can sometimes give the steel a yellow-green patina, while steel wool may produce a bit more of a brushed appearance.

Jill Marie Shulse
True Character, 2009
1.6 x 0.9 x 0.3 cm
Steel wire, antique level, optometrist lens, tin type, nickel, brass found object, brass screws; coiled, domed, etched
Photo by Dennis Schwartz

Robert Dancik
Cage Ring, 2009
7.3 x 4.5 x 3.6 cm
Steel wire, coral, wooden form; burned out
Photo by Paul Mounsey

• For chains with small links, rub the finished piece in the palms of your hands, wash the residue off your hands, and repeat until no black soot collects on your skin. Make sure to wash your hands often enough so you aren't redistributing the dirt back on the piece. (I learned this brilliant cleaning method—as I have many things in this book—from American jewelry artist Keith Lo Bue.)

At this stage, you'll see your work start to shine, literally. Actually, in the case of steel, you'll see a matte silver-gray luster. Beautiful!

Use Microcrystalline Wax to Finish

Steel must be finished to seal and protect it. I recommend a microcrystalline wax for its archival qualities. You'll want to rub a little on a rag and work it into all the surfaces of the cleaned, final piece. I've also used a toothbrush for extra-tight spots. (Another Keith Lo Bue tip is to melt a bit of wax into a hard-to-reach area by holding a butane lighter close to it. The lighter does the work for you. The wax will melt into the little space.)

A Word about the Order of the Day

I'm all about learning the rules, so I can be comfortable breaking them. For most projects, I work the wire in the order that the techniques in this chapter are listed: cut, straighten, form (curve, angle, forge, twist, and texture), file, and clean. But, as with most rules, there's an exception, and for steel wirework, it has to do with cleaning.

Cleaning is basically another form of handling the wire, and handling hardens wire. You can clean the wire before starting a piece, during fabrication, or after the jewelry is complete. If possible, wait until the end. Projects utilizing fragile, fine-gauge wire or complicated, tight-knit designs may require pre-cleaning, as cleanup in tight spots afterward is almost impossible. Try to work a balance with each piece. Will pre-cleaning harden the wire too much to work it the way you want? Would cleaning a fragile piece ruin its form? If you wait until the end, will you be able to work wax into the tight spots to keep the piece from rusting?

And really, don't fret about this too much. It's pretty hard to mess up. If you see a bit of the old orange nightmare—rust— cropping up at a later date, simply brush it off and re- seal the piece. (See? Rules ain't *all that*!)

TOOL KIT

CUTTING TOOLS

Heavy-duty flush cutter

Memory wire cutter

Standard cutter

Jeweler's saw & saw blades, size 3/0 or 2/0

FORMING TOOLS

Mallet, rawhide or plastic

Round-nose pliers

Forming pliers

Assorted mandrels or tubular objects

Flat-nose pliers

Vise

Bent-nose pliers

Standard hammer

Ball-peen hammer

Bench block

Power drill, power screwdriver,
or flexible shaft machine

FINISHING TOOLS

Medium hand file

Small needle files

Fine steel wool

Wire brushes

Microcrystalline wax

Rag

Hand cleaner

SAFETY TOOLS

Safety glasses

Safety gloves

Hearing protection

Dust mask

Jim Cotter
Ring with Steel & Amethyst, 2008
3.5 x 3 x 4 cm
Sterling silver, steel wire, cement,
amethyst; cast
Photo by artist

Ronna Sarvas Weltman
All the Rage, 2007
5.1 x 2.5 x 50.8 cm
Steel wire, polymer clay, shoe polish;
formed, textured, cured, stained
Photo by Doug Yaple

Lori Hawke-Ramin
The Color Lesson, 2007
Orange ring: 1.5 x 1 x 0.3 cm
Steel wire, cubic zirconia,
enamel; formed
Photo by artist

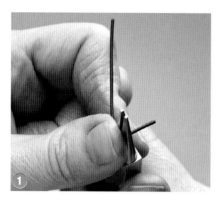

Besides knowing how to work the wire in simple ways, you need a few basic jewelry-making skills before diving into your first project. It's funny how these jewelry basics work. Designers use them so often they should become rote, but the techniques can often be challenging because each piece itself is new. The steps appear simple—and they are—but getting everything to work just right each time can include tiny frustrations. For example, creating the perfect plain loop (some of us are whacked-out traditionalists about this), is easy if you know a few simple little tricks.

Creating a Plain Loop

Plain loops (sometimes called eyes), are the hangers of jewelry making. Loops hold jump rings and dangle beads or charms. Plan ahead a bit when creating loops. Make them big enough so that the components they hold fit comfortably inside the loop with some allowance for movement.

1 Gently bend the wire down against a bead, an object, or your pliers to a 135-degree angle as shown in photo 1. (A 135-degree angle is half way between 90 degrees and 180 degrees.)

> **Note:** Most how-to sources say to bend the wire to a right angle (90 degrees), but I find that bending a slightly larger angle helps make the loop's "lollipop top," with the circle positioned straight up on its stick.

2 Cut the bent wire with flush cutters, leaving a ⅜-inch (1 cm) tail. This tail length works well if you are using 20- to 22-gauge wire and the inner diameter of the loop is fairly small. For heavier wire gauges, leave a longer tail; for lighter gauges, make the tail shorter.

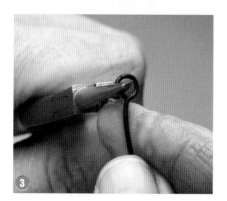

3 Grip the very end of the wire with the tip of the round-nose pliers. Roll the pliers toward you to form half the loop (photo 2).

④ Without taking the pliers away from the wire, ease your grip slightly, then roll the tips of the pliers back within the loop. Roll the pliers again to complete a tiny circle (photo 3).

⑤ Place the loop on a bench block, and hammer the wire to harden or texture it (photo 4). File the wire end smooth. Clean and finish the wire.

Creating a Wrapped Loop

A wrapped loop is the fancy city-cousin to the plain loop. It adds strength, security, and a decorative finish to your work.

① To create a placeholder for the wrap, grip the wire above the object to be held with the tip of flat-nose pliers. At the point precisely above the pliers, bend the wire down to a 135-degree angle as shown in photo 5.

② Grip the wire at the beginning of the bend with the tip of round-nose pliers. Form the wire up and around the pliers (photo 6).

Bryan S. Petersen
Boat Necklace, 2006
7 x 1.9 x 1.3 cm
Tin, street sign, steel
Photo by artist

Jennifer Wells
Ball Necklace, 2008
Longest: 92 cm
Steel wire, 14-karat gold, gold thread; wrapped
Photo by Dan DiCaprio

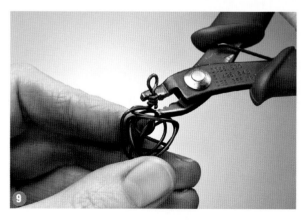

③ Ease your grip slightly and swing the pliers up to the top of the bend, where they will be out of the way of your next step. (The pliers should now be situated inside the loop you're forming). As shown in photo 7, re-grip the wire and complete the loop, positioning the wire ends at a 90-degree angle. Add any components to the loop at this point.

④ Using any type of pliers, grip the entire loop and hold it steady with your non-dominant hand as shown in photo 8. (Grip the loop away from the area to be wrapped.) If you have added a component, tip the piece downward at this point so the dangle is out of the way.

⑤ Grip the tail wire with a second pair of pliers and wrap it around the shank at the location saved in step 1. Wrap the wire in two half-way-around motions to fill the shank, keeping consecutive wraps close and tight. After each motion, re-grip the wire with the pliers. (You'll notice some errant bending—try to keep it contained to the end of the wire.)

⑥ When you have completed several wraps (only one is actually necessary; the rest fill in the gap and are decorative), use wire cutters to snip off the excess wire close to the coil.

⑦ Using pliers, carefully tuck the cut wire end close to the bottom of the coil. Crimping pliers works best for this step, if you have them handy (photo 9).

⑧ Place the loop on a bench block and hammer the wire to harden or texture it. File the wire end smooth. Clean and finish the wire.

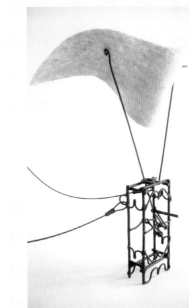

Gary Schott
Caress, 2006
Steel wire, cloth, silver;
formed, soldered
Photo by artist

Making Jump Rings

Jump rings are the paper clips of jewelry making. They connect one part to another, orient the direction an element faces, give energy and movement to jewelry, and can act as one end of a clasp.

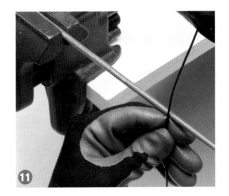

Making your own jump rings gives you carte blanche in their design and engineering (not to mention the independence you get from not having to rely on manufactured jump ring sizes, gauges, and metals). As shown in photo 10, you can make rings that are hefty or demure, thick or thin, as big or as little as you choose.

You can make jump rings by the few or by the dozen, but for the purposes of the projects in this book (where we're not making a chain-mail vest), let's go low-tech.

❶ Select a mandrel with a diameter that is equal to the interior diameter of the jump rings you wish to make. Lock the mandrel in a vise. Cut at least 12 inches (30.5 cm) of wire.

❷ Measure 6 inches (15.2 cm) from one end of the wire. Place the wire against one end of the mandrel at this point and hold it tightly with your thumb (photo 11).

Fabrizio Tridenti
Untitled, 2009
5 x 3.6 x 1.8 cm
Steel wire; folded, oxidized
Photo by artist

3 Hold the other end of the wire in your other hand. Coil the wire around the mandrel, consistently pulling the wire taut and positioning each coil as close to the last one as possible (photo 12).

> **Note:** As you apply pressure while turning, the end of the wire above your thumb will most likely diminish. If it hasn't, simply coil this end tight against the mandrel in the opposite direction.

4 Slide the coiled wire up the mandrel, positioning it next to the vise. Position a set of pliers (one that has a hole in the center) around the mandrel, and scoot them up to the other end of the coil. Holding the pliers tight, strike the closed jaws just below the mandrel with a hammer (photo 13). This blow will tighten any gaps between the coils. (This step also begins the hardening process.) Remove the mandrel from the vise and the coil from the mandrel.

5 Use flush cutters to remove the end of the wire that hasn't conformed to the mandrel. This is the first cut of the first jump ring. As shown in photo 14, flip the cutters so that the flush side is butted against the first cut end and clip the adjacent coil only, letting the ring fall onto your work surface. (This should form your first jump ring, a complete perfect circle.)

6 Inspect the ring and remove any burrs with a needle file.

7 Repeat steps 5 and 6 for the rest of the coil then clip off the final bit of waste wire at the end.

Opening & Closing Jump Rings & Loops

Opening, inserting, and closing jump rings around two or more elements is an especially easy way to connect jewelry components.

1 To open a jump ring, use two pairs of pliers to grasp each side of the ring at the cut. Slowly and simultaneously, move one cut end of the ring toward you and the other end away from you (photo 15). Do not pull apart the cut ends of the jump ring, as this will ruin the shape of the ring and weaken or break the wire.

2 To close a jump ring, reverse the same movements described in step 1 until the ends meet. To get the cut ends to align perfectly, bypass the ends slightly (you will feel them touching when you are close); the metal's springiness will cause them to move back into proper alignment.

33

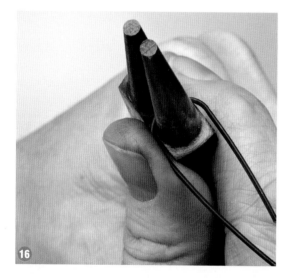

16

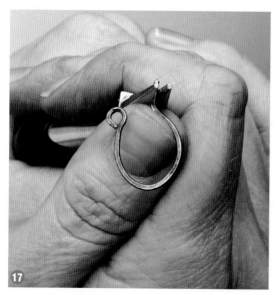

17

Forming Ear Wires

Ear wires can be designed with as much or as little flair as you choose. Some earring designs are simply fancy-schmancy ear wires! But whether you want the traditional, utilitarian sort or the impressively left-of-center type, the same techniques apply. The steps below outline the traditional ear wire design, but adapt them as you see fit.

❶ Starting with a 3-inch (7.6 cm) length of wire (or more; this is where the fancy part comes in), use round-nose pliers to bend a small, plain loop with an inner dimension of 2 or 3 mm. This will be the connection for the rest of your earring.

❷ Working on the opposite side of the wire with the largest part of your round-nose or forming pliers, slowly form a curve above the small loop made in step 1 (photo 16). Making a series of tiny rounded bends will form a smooth, continuous curve that fits comfortably in your earlobe.

❸ Leave the remaining wire length straight, so it extends down past the plain loop (or not; see the circular style in photo 17).

❹ With flat-nose pliers, bend a jaunty outward angle near the end of the wire as shown in photo 17, approximately ⅜ inch (1 cm) from the bottom. (This little angle makes inserting the wire into the ear a snap!) Clip off any excess wire.

❺ Hammer the loop to harden it, and file the end of the ear wire smooth. Clean and finish the wire.

❻ Repeat all steps, as you obviously need to make ear wires in pairs!

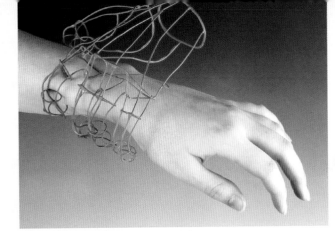

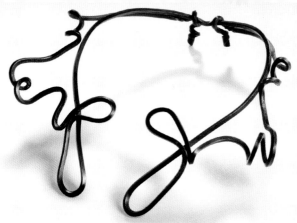

Jason Tobiansky
Grip, 2006
14 x 12 x 7 cm
Steel wire, plastic tool dip; formed, soldered, dipped
Photo by artist

Jaclyn Davidson
Untitled, 2009
Wire length: 457.2 cm
Steel; forged
Photo by Michael Heeney

Amy Tavern
Scallop Link Necklace, 2009
83.8 x 1.3 x 2.5 cm
Mild steel, 18-karat yellow gold; formed,
soldered, forged
Photo by Hank Drew

Francis Willemstijn
Ground, 2004
40 cm in diameter
Silver wire, 17th century coin and buttons, iron,
wood, gold, horn
Photo by artist

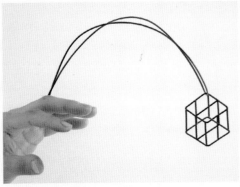

Motoko Furuhashi
Untitled, 2009
10 x 18 x 9 cm
Steel wire; fabricated
Photo by artist

Merav Goldschmidt-Kay
Wedding Rings, 2007
Largest: 0.7 x 2.5 x 2.5 cm
Steel wire, copper; hand fabricated
Photo by Dror Arinun

35

projects

I f you've never worked with steel wire before, let me introduce you to
a medium that makes a lasting impression! This material, with its dead
soft handling and inexpensive price, is a treat to get to know. Use these
12 earring styles as an exercise in familiarizing yourself with steel wire's
amenable—dare I say easily manipulated?—nature.

MEET 'N' GREET

Giraffe's Eyelashes

1 Cut 4 inches (10.2 cm) of 16-gauge steel wire.

2 Use round-nose pliers to form a plain loop at one end of the wire.

3 Slightly curve the wire with your fingers.

4 Hammer the wire, forging the middle section to emphasize the fullest part of the curve.

5 Repeat steps 1 through 4 to make the second earring.

6 Create a pair of simple ear wires and connect one to each earring.

7 File the wire ends, clean the earrings, and finish them with wax.

Cowlick

1 Cut seven pieces of 19-gauge steel wire, each 3 to 4 inches (7.6 to 10.2 cm) long. Slightly curve the wires with your fingers.

2 Use round-nose pliers to form a plain loop at the top of each cut wire.

3 Cut 2 inches (5.1 cm) of 19-gauge steel wire. Form a jump ring with an inside diameter of approximately ¼ inch (6 mm). Hammer the jump ring.

4 Hammer each wire length, forging the ends so the tips splay out.

5 Open a jump ring. Add all the curved components, and close the loop.

6 Repeat steps 1 through 5 to make the second earring.

7 Create a pair of ear wires and connect one to each earring. File the wire ends, clean the earrings, and finish them with wax.

MATERIALS & TOOLS

■ **STEEL WIRE, 16, 19, AND 28 GAUGE**
■ **TOOL KIT, PAGE 27**

AUTHOR'S NOTES

■ I TEND TO FAVOR BOLDER, LARGER-SCALED DESIGNS. SOME STYLES IN THIS EARRING COLLECTION MEASURE UP TO 4 INCHES (10.2 CM) LONG AND 2 INCHES (5.1 CM) WIDE. ADJUST THE SIZES TO FIT YOUR PERSONAL PREFERENCE.

■ ALL OF THE EARRING PROJECTS ARE COMPLEMENTED WITH 19-GAUGE (OR THINNER) HANDMADE EAR WIRES. SIMPLE INSTRUCTIONS FOR MAKING YOUR OWN EAR WIRES CAN BE FOUND ON PAGE 34.

MEET 'N' GREET

Giant's Ring, Giant's Teardrop & Wee People Gourd

1 For each design you wish to make, cut two lengths of 16-gauge steel wire, each 6 inches (15.2 cm) or less.

2 Following the directions below, form the steel wire around a mandrel or other cylindrical object. The diameter of the mandrel will be the inside diameter of the earring.

For the Giant's Ring

Form the midsection of the wire fully around the mandrel, then form a plain loop on one end.

For the Giant's Teardrop

Form the midsection of the wire halfway around the mandrel, extending the tails into a point and leaving one end ¼ inch (6 mm) longer. Form a plain loop on the longer wire end.

For the Wee People Gourd

Form the midsection of the wire three-quarters of the way around the mandrel, straightening the wires upward from this point. Form a plain loop at each wire end.

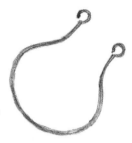

3 Hammer the steel wire shape:

For the Giant's Ring and the Wee People Gourd

Use a ball-peen hammer.

For the Giant's Teardrop

Use a standard hammer and a flathead screwdriver to add texture to the wire. Place the tip of the screwdriver on the wire and hammer its handle. Gradually move and strike the screwdriver to create the radial pattern. Using two pairs of pliers, orient the loop by bending the wire into a 90-degree angle.

4 Repeat steps 2 and 3 to make the second earring for each pair.

5 Create a pair of ear wires for each set of earrings. Connect the wires to the earrings.

For the Wee People Gourd

For each ear wire, cut 2 inches (5.1 cm) of 19-gauge wire. Make an abbreviated ear hook by first forming the wire over a mandrel. Create a plain loop at one end and a jaunty angle at the other end. Open the plain loop on the hook, feed it through the plain loop on the earring, and close.

6 File the wire ends, clean the earrings, and finish them with wax.

Geo-metrics: Hexagon

1 Cut a 6-inch (15.2 cm) length of 16-gauge steel wire.

2 Make slight but distinct bends in the wire at precise 1-inch (2.5 cm) intervals.

3 Hammer the wire form to harden it.

4 Use two pairs of flat-tipped pliers to finesse the bends in a hexagon shape. Then, to make the gap between the wire's ends as tight as possible, work the wire ends back and forth as you would to close a jump ring.

5 Repeat steps 1 through 4 to make the second earring. Create a pair of ear wires, and connect the wires to the earrings.

6 File the wire ends, clean the earrings, and finish them with wax.

Geo-Metrics: Bursting Rectangle

1 Cut 7 inches (17.8 cm) of 16-gauge wire.

2 Make bends at points that are 1 inch (2.5 cm), 3 inches (7.6 cm), 4 inches (10.2 cm), and 5 inches (12.7 cm) away from one wire end. Once the rectangle is formed, the ends of the wire will overlap

3 Use a ball-peen hammer to harden the wire form.

4 Cut 12 inches (30.5 cm) of 28-gauge steel wire. Use this thin wire to tightly bind the overlapping ends. Pinch the ends of the binding wire with crimping pliers to hide them.

5 Repeat steps 1 through 4 to make the second earring. Create a pair of ear wires, and connect the wires to the earrings.

6 File the wire ends, clean the earrings, and finish them with wax.

MEET 'N' GREET

Scraper Tool

1 Cut 6½ inches (16.5 cm) of 19-gauge steel wire. Bend the wire to create the scraper tool shape shown.

2 Use round-nose pliers to form a plain loop at wire end A (see drawing).

3 Cut and discard any extra wire, then bend a jaunty angle at the other end, fitting it through the plain loop made in step 2.

4 Hammer the earring to harden the wire.

Note: This style of earring relies on spring-tight hardening. You'll need to work the wire longer than other styles to make sure the closure works and will afford continued wear and use.

5 Repeat steps 1 through 4 to make the second earring. File the wire ends, clean the earrings, and finish them with wax.

He Loves Me

1 Cut 10 inches (25.4 cm) of 16-gauge steel wire.

2 Form double-back curves to make the five-petal flower. To accomplish this, alternate bending the wire around a pen or a mandrel and the tip of a pair of round-nose pliers. Slightly overlap the wire ends, then cut and discard any extra wire.

3 Hammer the flower shape to harden the wire.

4 Cut 12 inches (30.5 cm) of 28-gauge steel wire. Tightly wrap this wire around the overlapping ends of the flower shape. With crimping pliers, pinch the ends of the binding wire to hide them.

5 Repeat steps 1 through 4 to make the second earring. Create a pair of ear wires and connect them to the earrings.

6 File the wire ends, clean the earrings, and finish them with wax.

Penmanship Practice

1 Cut 10 inches (25.4 cm) of 16-gauge steel wire. Use round-nose pliers to form a plain loop at one end of the wire.

2 Approximately ½ inch (1.3 cm) from the plain loop, bend a loop around the largest part of a pair of round-nose pliers. Repeat this process to shape the rest of the wire. If needed, cut off any excess wire.

3 Hammer the wire shape to harden it, using less pressure at points where the wire overlaps.

④ Repeat steps 1 through 3 to make the second earring. Create a pair of ear wires and connect them to the earrings.

⑤ File the wire ends, clean the earrings, and finish them with wax.

Smokestack

① Cut 24 inches (61 cm) of 19-gauge steel wire. Slightly harden the wire by passing it through steel wool or a green kitchen scrub pad.

② Wind the wire willy-nilly (important technical term) around a pen or a mandrel with a ⅜-inch (1 cm) diameter. Remove the wire from the mandrel. Pull and poke the wire until you have created a satisfyingly chaotic shape.

③ Pull one wire end out of the wound shape. Use round-nose pliers to form a plain loop on this end. Hammer the plain loop to harden it.

④ Repeat steps 1 through 3 to make the second earring. Make a pair of ear wires, and connect them to the earrings.

⑤ File the wire ends, clean the earrings, and finish them with wax.

String Art

① Cut 12 inches (30.5 cm) of 16-gauge wire. Bend and overlap the wire until you get the amorphous shape you desire (see drawing).

② Hammer the piece with a ball-peen hammer, using less pressure at the overlapped points.

③ Make the second earring and a pair of ear wires. Connect the wires to the earrings.

④ File the wire ends, clean the earrings, and finish them with wax.

MATERIALS & TOOLS

▪ **STEEL WIRE, 19 GAUGE**
▪ **BRASS WIRE, 16 GAUGE**
▪ **TOOL KIT, PAGE 27**
▪ **DESIGN TEMPLATE, PAGE 127**

With this project you're signing up for a little jump ring boot camp. This snazzy, jump-ring (99 percent jump ring, 1 percent toggle bar) project utilizes wire of various gauges and metal types. It's super easy and oh-so-fun! No soldering required!

PRACTICE MAKES PERFECT

1 Cut 9 inches (22.9 cm) of 16-gauge steel wire. Create three jump rings using a cylinder or mandrel that will yield 1-inch (2.5 cm) inside diameters. (I used my jeweler's saw handle, but the right kitchen tool will work just fine.)

2 Cut 18 inches (45.7 cm) of 16-gauge steel wire. Create 15 jump rings with ½-inch (1.3 cm) inside diameters.

3 Cut 24 inches (61 cm) of 16-gauge steel wire. Create 33 jump rings with ⅜-inch (1 cm) inside diameters.

4 Lay out the jump rings to form a bib necklace as shown in the template.

5 Cut 18 inches (45.7 cm) of 16-gauge steel wire. Create 35 to 40 jump rings with ⅛-inch (3 mm) inside diameters.

6 Cut 18 inches (45.7 cm) of 16-gauge brass wire. Create 30 jump rings with ⅛-inch (3 mm) inside diameters.

7 File and hammer all jump rings. Assemble the necklace, opening and closing the jump rings with two pairs of pliers.

8 Cut 2 inches (5.1 cm) of 16-gauge steel wire. In the midsection, form a plain loop and make a bar toggle as shown in the detail, top right. Hammer the bar, using less pressure at the overlapped points. Forge the ends. Attach the bar to the necklace with a jump ring.

9 Clamp one point of the necklace triangle in a padded vice, holding it taut at another point. Clean the taut section of the necklace with a brass brush. Reposition the necklace as needed so you can clean all areas in this way. Finish and seal the necklace with wax.

Wear this urban-dreamcatcher-meets-prehistoric-body-adornment as a funky talisman against negativity. The really cool thing is that this necklace can never be worn the same way twice; the way it has been engineered, it will lay on your neck differently every time.

STICKS & STONES

Forming the Wire Components

1 Cut 23 pieces of 16-gauge steel wire, varying the length of each from 2 to 5 inches (5.1 to 12.7 cm). File the wire ends and form a plain loop at one end of each wire.

2 Add a fossil to five wires that are at least 3 inches (7.6 cm) long. Form a plain loop at the other end of each of these five wires. Bend a slight curve in each wire component (see drawing).

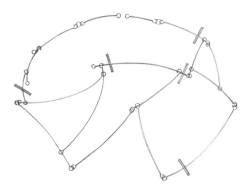

3 Hammer each wire component to harden it, carefully working around the fossils. Set aside two 2-inch (5.1 cm) components.

Creating the Toggle Clasp

1 Cut two 2-inch (5.1 cm) lengths of 16-gauge wire. File the wire ends.

2 To form the toggle end of the clasp, bend one end of one 2-inch (5.1 cm) wire completely around a ½-inch (1.3 cm) mandrel and bend the other end completely around the tip of round-nose pliers, forming an S shape (see project photo).

3 To make the bar end of the clasp, center the tip of the round-nose pliers on the remaining 2-inch (5.1 cm) wire length. Bend

each wire end all the way around one of the pliers' jaws, so the ends bypass each other and extend out in opposite directions. Curve the extended wire ends in the direction of the loop. Forge each end of the bar.

4 Create two jump rings around an ⅛-inch (3 mm) mandrel. Hammer the rings to harden them.

Assembling the Necklace

1 To form a chain, attach the looped wire end of a component to the straight end of another component. Build the chain from the center out, using and varying the larger components first. Continue until the necklace measures approximately 20 inches (50.8 cm).

2 Cut two 2-inch (5.1 cm) lengths of 16-gauge steel wire. File the ends, and form a plain loop on each end.

3 Use jump rings to attach one 2-inch (5.1 cm) wire segment to the last component on each side of the necklace. Attach one piece of the clasp to the other end of each wire segment.

4 Drape the piece onto the dress form or neck mandrel. Randomly add the remaining wire components to the necklace to enhance or smooth any areas that jut out. Utilize a pleasing placement of the fossils as visual focal points; you may need to re-orient the loops.

5 Clean the necklace and finish it with wax.

MATERIALS & TOOLS

- STEEL WIRE, 16 GAUGE
- 5 CRINOIDS STEM PIECES
- TOOL KIT, PAGE 27
- DRESS FORM OR NECK MANDREL

D id you know that by using steel wire, you're saving the world? After all, green isn't just a color anymore; it's an ecologic state of mind! Choosing the very economical steel wire —instead of a precious metal like silver or gold—means you're aiding the world recycling effort and reducing your carbon footprint. In your own little way, you're a global hero.

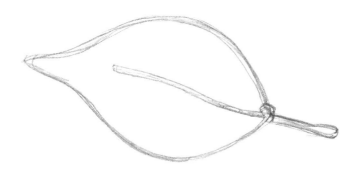

MATERIALS & TOOLS

■ **STEEL WIRE, 16, 19, AND 28 GAUGE**

■ **TOOL KIT, PAGE 27**

WHEN GRAY IS GREEN

Shaping the Leaf

1 Cut 12 inches (30.5 cm) of 16-gauge steel wire. With round-nose pliers, form a fold 1 inch (2.5 cm) from one wire end. (The wire now has a U-shape at one end.)

2 To form the stem, double-back another 1 inch (2.5 cm). (The wire now has an S-shape at one end.) Form the remainder of the wire into a leaf shape.

3 As shown in the drawing, wrap the wire tail around the point where the leaf and stem meet. Continue on to form the midrib (center line), ending approximately 1 inch (2.5 cm) from the tip of the leaf. Forge this wire end.

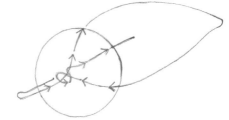

4 Hammer the wire leaf with a ball-peen hammer, using less force at the over-lapped points.

Forming & Attaching the Pin Finding

1 Cut 4 inches (10.2 cm) of 19-gauge steel wire. With round-nose pliers, form a complete loop in the wire that is 2 inches (5.1 cm) from one end.

2 Double-back the wire to run parallel another 1⅞ inches (4.8 cm). At this point, use flat-nose pliers to bend a right angle in the wire. Near this angle, use the tip of the round-nose pliers to bend a 45-degree angle ⅜-inch (1 cm) from one end of the wire. Cut the wire ⅛ inch (3 mm) beyond the bend.

3 Use needle files to file the pin stem to a sharp point. File the other wire end flat, clean the pin finding, and finish it with wax.

4 Cut a 6-inch (15.2 cm) piece of 28-gauge steel wire. Use this wire to bind the pin finding, fastener side away from the piece, to the midrib of the leaf.

5 Tuck in the ends of the binding wire with crimping pliers. Clean and finish these connections as you did the other parts of the brooch.

A new idea for a stacked bangle can appear anywhere. You could be down at the lake house, looking for a lure in the tackle box, and POW...inspiration hits. You collect some treasures and create jewelry instead, making a bad fishing day much, much better. Cold connections make putting this piece together a snap.

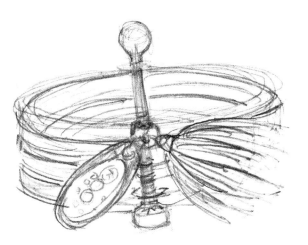

FINDERS KEEPERS

Forming the Bangles

❶ Cut six pieces of 16-gauge steel wire, each 12 inches (30.5 cm) long.

❷ Forge ½ inch (1.3 cm) of one end of each of the six wires. Form loops on both ends of the wires that will accommodate the hinge pin you have selected.

❸ Form each of the wire pieces around a mandrel that is large enough to accommodate the widest part of your hand.

❹ Hammer each bangle to harden the wire. File the wire ends, clean the bangles, and finish them with wax.

Assembling the Bangle

❶ Thread several washers or nuts onto the hinge pin. Feed the bangles on, interspersing them with more washers and nuts as desired.

❷ Add the ring charm or a similar finding to the hinge pin. Add the remaining bangle components (including the fishing lure) and several more washers/nuts, leaving ⅛ to ¼ inch (3 to 6 mm) above the last hardware piece to accept the decorative nut (see drawing).

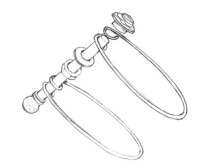

❸ Mix a tiny bit of epoxy putty according to the manufacturer's directions. Insert the putty into the nut and the nut onto the top of the hinge pin. Wipe away any extra putty and put aside to dry overnight. (Note: Epoxy putty will harden like cement. Make sure to place your components exactly where you want them to be as they are drying.)

MATERIALS & TOOLS

■ STEEL WIRE, 16 GAUGE

■ VINTAGE DOOR HINGE PIN, 2⅜ INCHES (6 CM)

■ 4 TO 8 ASSORTED NUTS AND WASHERS

■ RING CHARM OR SIMILAR FINDING

■ FISHING LURE, HOOK REMOVED

■ DECORATIVE NUT OR OTHER SMALL FINIAL/TOPPER

■ EPOXY PUTTY

■ TOOL KIT, PAGE 27

49

Here's a new twist to an old wire—use your favorite found object as the focal point and closure on a twisted wire bracelet. Encompass just about anything you can get your wire around and create a custom loop finish. It's such a fun and easy concept, you'll create an armload. Get creative and invent your own new look—a little bit Steampunk, a little bit Goth, and a little bit junk drawer. Now that's what I call twisted!

TWIST ON A TWIST

MATERIALS & TOOLS

- STEEL WIRE, 16 GAUGE
- FOUND OBJECT, 1 INCH (2.5 CM) OR SMALLER
- EPOXY PUTTY
- TOOL KIT, PAGE 27
- POWER DRILL WITH ADJUSTABLE CHUCK
- VISE

Forming the Wire Clasp

1 Cut 36 inches (91.4 cm) of 16-gauge steel wire. Determine the final orientation of the found-object clasp.

2 At its midpoint, form the wire into a clasp shape that fits around the found object. (For example, my clasp shape is a square that complements and fits over the die.) Twist the wire once at the connecting point.

3 Hammer the wire clasp shape to harden it.

Twisting the Wire

1 Position the found object inside the wire clasp. Place the clasp in the end of a lined vise so the remaining wire extends out one side. Tighten the vise.

2 Hold the wire ends together, insert them in a power drill chuck, and tighten with a chuck key. Slowly power the drill to twist the wire. Continue twisting the wire until the desired degree of tightness is obtained.

3 Determine the finished length of the bracelet, then add ½ to 1 inch (1.3 to 2.5 cm). Cut the twisted wire to this length.

4 Form a hook with the last ½ inch (1.3 cm) of the wire end. File, clean, and finish the wire with wax.

Adding the Found-Object Clasp

1 Mark the end of the found object that will receive the wire end, and drill this point with a ⅛-inch (3 mm) bit. Make sure the hole will be low enough on the object to fit inside the bend, which will act as a stop when the clasp is closed.

2 Check the fit of the wire clasp and adjust if necessary. Following the manufacturer's instructions, glue the found object to the wire end with epoxy putty. Let the glue dry overnight.

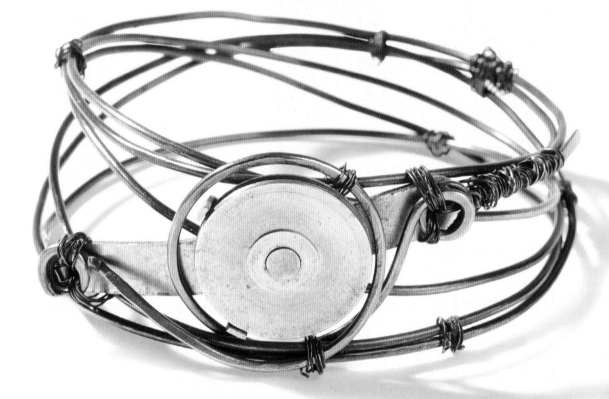

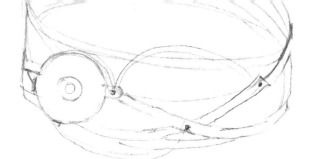

This odd title refers to an order-out-of-chaos wire technique, *not* the late-60s TV show starring the big yellow dragon-mayor surnamed H.R. Pufnstuf. When one has a wide paw, one needs an oversized object to form bangles and cuffs around. Simply use the perimeter of (yes, you guessed it) a hockey puck, wrap strategic points with binding wire, and futz with the shape until it's pleasing to the eye. (For you little-handed folk, the title could be Grape Jam Jar 'n Futz or Tuna Can 'n Futz!)

PUCK 'N' FUTZ

Forming the Bangle

1 Cut 60 inches (1.5 m) of 16-gauge steel wire. File and forge each wire end. Use round-nose pliers to bend a narrow U-shape ½ inch (1.3 cm) from one end.

2 Insert this curved wire end into a hole in the dial apparatus (or wire component). Crimp the end of the curved wire to the wire beneath it.

3 Lay the steel wire against the puck and turn the dial out of the way. Tightly wind the entire wire length in a random, overlapping fashion. Turn the dial so it stands perpendicular to the curved wire end.

4 Form another narrow, U-shaped bend at the other end of the wire where it meets the remaining dial hole. Fit the bent wire through the hole then crimp its end flat to the wire. Remove the puck from the wound wire. Adjust the shape of the wire as needed to stabilize the piece.

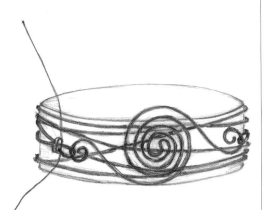

MATERIALS & TOOLS

▪ **STEEL WIRE, 16 AND 28 GAUGE**

▪ **FOUND-OBJECT DIAL OR 12 TO 24 INCHES (30.5 TO 61 CM) OF 16-GAUGE STEEL WIRE***

▪ **TOOL KIT, PAGE 27**

▪ **HOCKEY PUCK OR OTHER ROUND OBJECT WITH PERIMETER MEASUREMENT EQUAL TO THE BANGLE'S DESIRED INTERIOR DIMENSION**

*DON'T HAVE A DIAL APPARATUS LYING AROUND? FORM YOUR OWN FOCAL COMPONENT FROM 16-GAUGE STEEL WIRE BY CREATING A SPIRAL CENTER AND LOOPING THE WIRE ENDS AS SHOWN IN THE DRAWING BELOW, LEFT.

PUCK 'N' FUTZ

⑤ Cut four to six pieces of 28-gauge steel wire, each 4 inches (10.2 cm) long. Identify several points on the bangle where two or three wires meet. To bind the bangle at these points, center a length of thin wire over them, tightly wrap it around twice, and then twist the ends of the binding wire, twist-tie style. This forms little wire slubs or bundles.

⑥ Hammer the bangle around a bracelet mandrel or metal pipe, taking care to avoid hitting the slubs. Clean the piece, and finish it with wax.

Embellishing the Focal Point

❶ Cut a 14-inch (35.6 cm) length of 16-gauge steel wire. Bend a circle in the center of the wire. The diameter of the circle should be slightly larger than the diameter of the dial. (I used a screwdriver handle as a mandrel.)

❷ At the ends of the 16-gauge wire, bend two smaller circles that are just a bit larger than the holes in the dial apparatus.

❸ Curve and hammer the circular component. File the wire ends and clean the piece.

❹ Cut two 9-inch (22.9 cm) lengths of 28-gauge wire. Secure the circular component to the bangle using a figure-eight wrap through each dial hole. File and clean the wire ends. Finish the piece with wax.

Visual artists tend to repeat certain images and motifs in their collective works. Dali painted "soft" clocks, elephants, and eggs; Escher drew birds, fish, reptiles, and staircases. Alexander Calder's jewelry motifs are simple, clean, and (how surprising) linear. But nowhere in his oeuvre is a single necklace that incorporates such a bounty of his favorite motifs—until now. In honor of this genius of wire, here is The All-Calder Revue Necklace: An Iron-Clad Retrospective.

THE ALL-CALDER REVUE

Forming the Motifs

1 Cut the following pieces of 19-gauge steel wire:

- one piece, 36 inches (91.4 cm) long, for the flower

- two pieces, each 12 inches (30.5 cm) long, for the leaves

- two pieces, each 24 inches (61 cm) long, for the flat spirals

- two pieces, each 9 inches (22.9 cm) long, for the boomerangs

- two pieces, each 12 inches (30.5 cm) long, for the cone spirals

2 Working from the center of the wire, form the flower petals as shown in the drawing below. Twist each petal at its base and leave a 1½-inch-long (3.8 cm) tail at each end of the wire. Twist the ends at the base of the flower to secure it.

3 Use round-nose pliers to form (clockwise from top) the wire leaf, spiral, boomerang, and cone motifs. At the top of the boomerang shape, twist the wire connection point twice to secure.

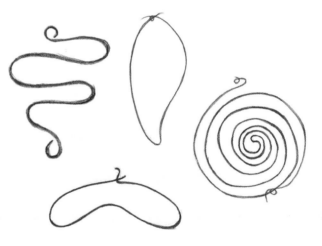

4 Hammer each of the wire motifs and their tails.

5 From the tail of each wire motif, form a loose coil using a ⅛-inch (3 mm) mandrel. Each coil will act as a bail.

6 Clean each wire motif and finish them with wax. Using the tip of round-nose pliers, push the centers of the cone spirals into cone shapes.

Forming the Meandering Clasp

1 Cut two pieces of 19-gauge steel wire:

- one piece, 5½ inches (14 cm) long, for the meandering end
- one piece, 2 inches (5.1 cm) long, for the S-toggle end

2 Using the project photo as a guide, form both clasp shapes with round-nose pliers, then hammer to harden the wire. Clean the clasp components and finish them with wax.

Forming the Connecting "Grubs"

1 Cut two 6-inch (15.2 cm) pieces of 19-gauge steel wire.

2 Coil one piece tightly around a 2-mm mandrel 10 times. Trim, leaving a ⅜-inch (1 cm) length. Form this leftover length into a plain loop perpendicular to the coil.

3 Repeat step 2 to form a second connecting "grub," clean the pair, and finish them with wax.

Assembling the Necklace

1 Open and close the plain loop of one connector "grub" around each clasp half.

2 Fit a "grub" onto one leather cord end. Hammer its coils on a slant to hold the cording in place. Repeat to the other side.

Some living things "bloom" at night: bats, opossum, and naked mole rats, to name a few. Nocturnal flowers and a crescent moon were chosen for this bracelet. "Drawing" these shapes is easy by shaping dead-soft, thin-gauge wire with your fingers—so much so that you may be inspired to capture your own nightlife in a wire pendant. How about a wombat, Gila monster, or cuttlefish? No?

MATERIALS & TOOLS

- **STEEL WIRE, 19, AND 28 GAUGE**
- **CRYSTAL MOON PENDANT, 30 MM**
- **JUMP RING, ¼ INCH (6 MM), GUNMETAL FINISH**
- **LOBSTER CLASP, ¼ INCH (6 MM), GUNMETAL FINISH**
- **TOOL KIT, PAGE 27**
- **JAR, CAN, OR BRACELET MANDREL**

GARDEN NOIR

Creating the Flower Components

1 Cut four pieces of 19-gauge steel wire, each 24 inches (61 cm) long. Cut four pieces of 28-gauge steel wire, each 12 inches (30.5 cm) long.

2 Form each flower from the 19-gauge wire lengths, using the drawings below as a guide.

3 Bind each flower's connecting points with a length of 28-gauge wire. Hide the ends.

4 Hammer the flower components lightly, avoiding the bound areas. Forge the stem ends.

5 File the ends of the wire, and finish the pieces with wax. Note: To retain the wire's blackest color, cleaning is omitted.

6 With your hands or a mallet, slightly curve each flower inward. Bending them over a jar or can also works well.

Creating the Crescent Moon Charm

1 Cut a piece of 28-gauge steel wire, 24 inches (30.5 cm) long.

2 Wrap one end of the wire around round-nose pliers three times, and position the loop at the top of the pendant. Then feed the wire through the pendant hole and continue to wrap the wire willy nilly around the pendant, ending at the top and leaving a 2-inch (5.1 cm) tail.

3 Wrap the tail around the neck of the wire loop and hide the end. Set aside.

Assembling the Bracelet

1 Form a loop with a ¼-inch (6 mm) inner diameter on each flower stem. Line up the wire flowers.

2 Attach the stem loop from one flower to a petal in another flower, until three of the flowers are connected. Connect the fourth with the stem to the inside.

3 Using the jump ring, attach the crescent moon charm and the clasp to the fourth flower's outermost petal.

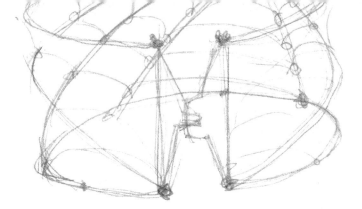

MATERIALS & TOOLS

- STEEL WIRE, 16, 18, AND 28 GAUGE
- FLY BROOCH, 1¼ INCHES (3.2 CM) LONG
- JEWELED SPIDER TIE TACK, ⅝ INCH (1.6 CM) LONG
- TOOL KIT, PAGE 27
- JAR, CAN, OR BRACELET MANDREL

A dream world for flies would have mountains of stinky rubble, farm fields with fence-to-fence cattle, and sunglasses built for a zillion eyes. But the pièce de résistance, the fly mother-of all-pies-in-the-sky, would be a football-field-size web that traps every spider who ever sat beside her. Let's try a version for the wrist!

FLIES HAVE DREAMS, TOO

Forming the Cuff Armature

1. Cut two pieces of 16-gauge steel wire, each 7 inches (17.8 cm) long. Cut two pieces of 16-gauge steel wire, each 3 inches (7.6 cm) long.

2. File the ends of the wires. Form a plain loop at each wire end that can lay flat. Hammer the wires to harden them.

3. Form a rectangle by opening the loops on the shorter wires and closing them around the longer wires. Keep the loops on the long wires oriented to the inside of the loops on the shorter wires.

4. Cut five pieces of 16-gauge steel wire, one each of the following lengths:

   • 3¾ inches (9.5 cm)

   • 2½ inches (6.4 cm)

   • 3¾ inches (9.5 cm)

   • 4½ inches (11.4 cm)

   • 4¾ inches (12.1 cm)

5. File, then form a plain loop on all wire ends. Hammer the wires to harden. In the order they are listed in step 4, attach each wire—side by side and by one loop—to one long side of the wire rectangle made in step 3. Position the wires 2½ inches (6.4 cm) from the bottom left corner of the rectangle.

Tip: To allow for ease of movement, bend the bottom loops so they remain perpendicular to the longer side of the rectangle. These wires will be the main spokes of the spider web.

6. Form a radial pattern of spokes by attaching the free loop ends to the other long side of the rectangle in this order: the leftmost wire at the upper left corner; the next wire 2¼ inches (5.7 cm) from the same corner; the third wire 3⅝ inches (9.2 cm) from the corner; and the fourth wire 5¼ inches (13.3 cm) from the same corner. Attach the fifth wire onto the right, short side of the rectangle, ⅝ inch (1.6 cm) down from the upper right corner.

FLIES HAVE DREAMS, TOO

Forming the Clasp

1 Cut one 4-inch (10.2 cm) length and one 5-inch (12.7 cm) length of 16-gauge steel wire. Using the drawing below (right) as a guide, form the loop end of the clasp half with the 4-inch (10.2 cm) length and the hook end with the 5-inch (12.7 cm) length. Add a plain loop to each end of the wire lengths. Hammer the clasp pieces. Bend a hook in the hook clasp half.

2 Position the narrow end of one part of the clasp in a lined vise. Tighten the vise. Reorient the loops' positions to be perpendicular to the rest of the length and become the clasp's "feet." Repeat the process for the other half of the clasp.

3 Following the drawing below, attach each part of the clasp to the *outside* of the loops on the short ends of the rectangle. The entire wire structure should be able to lay flat. Clean the wire structure.

4 Form the wire structure around a jar, can, or bracelet mandrel to form the cuff.

Building the Webbing & Adding the Bugs

1 Cut two 3-foot (91.4 cm) lengths of 18-gauge steel wire. Fasten the end of one wire near the bottom left-hand corner of the cuff.

2 Loop the wire counter-clockwise around each spoke on the cuff, bringing the wire in from underneath, then over and around, before moving on to the next spoke. To move to the next level, coil the wire clockwise around the cuff's bottom edge (see drawing).

3 Using the second wire length, wrap the upper left and right corners of the cuff. Hide the ends. Clean the wire web. Finish the entire cuff with wax.

4 Cut 12 inches (30.5 cm) of 28-gauge steel wire. Use wire cutters to remove the pin from the back of the spider tie tack. File as needed. Wire wrap the spider near the top right corner of the cuff. Trim any excess wire and hide the ends. Pin the fly brooch near the center of a radial wire.

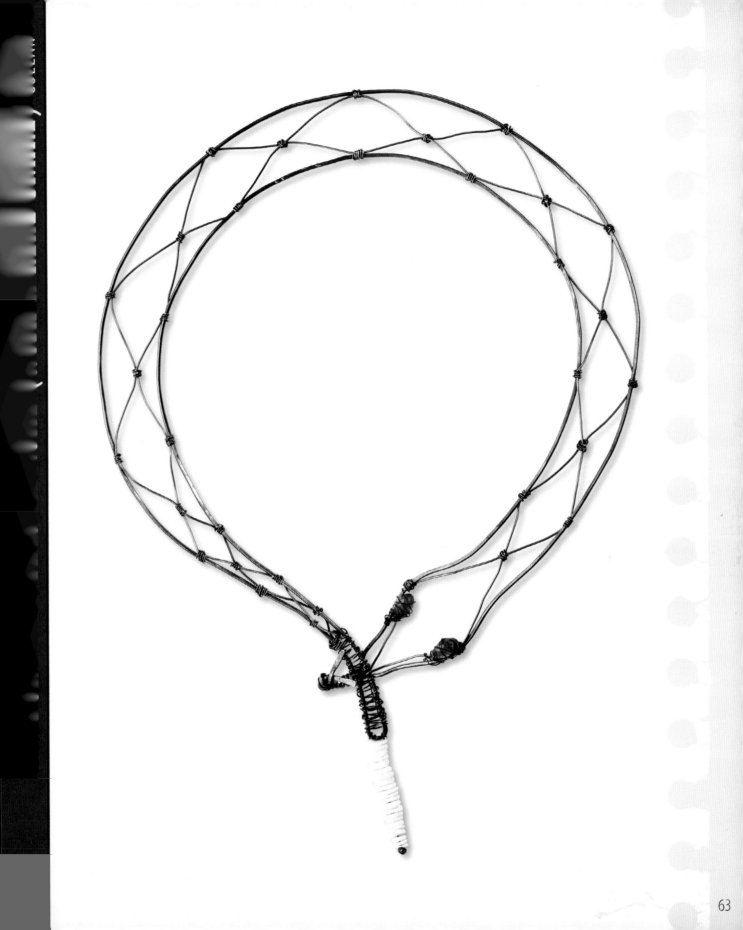

S nake handlers make me nervous; snake charmers are spellbinding (emphasis on the binding). Using your shoulders as a snake hanger leaves me speechless. Try fashioning (and accessorizing with) this daring rattler neckpiece instead. It's amazingly easy to construct, with just a few gauges of steel wire, some twists and turns, and a little shaping. It's also a lot less dangerous.

DON'T TRY THIS AT HOME (WITH A REAL SNAKE)

Forming the Snake Neckpiece

1 Cut a 5-foot (1.52 m) length of 16-gauge steel wire. Fold the wire in half and shape the snake's outline, beginning with the doubled wire forming the blunted tip of the tail and ending at the point of the nose.

2 As shown in the design template, twist the wire ends at the tip of the nose until the twisted wire measures 2 inches (5.1 cm). This is the snake's tongue. Allow the wire ends to separate slightly and cut the tips to ¼ inch (6 mm).

3 Hammer the outline of the wire snake and its tongue. Forge the ends of the tongue and file them. Bend the end of the tongue into a U-shaped curve. (This creates the closure that will "bite" the snake's tail.)

Adding the Diamond Pattern

1 Cut 8 feet (2.43 m) of 19-gauge steel wire and fold it in half. Anchor the fold just above the tongue and twist the ends twice tightly behind it.

2 Cut 36 lengths of 28-gauge steel wire, each 2 inches (5.1 cm). Form the 19-gauge wire into diamond shapes that fit inside the snake's outline. Start the first diamond inside the head by extending both wire ends to the head's widest point. Anchor each point with a 28-gauge wire length forming the beginning of a tight coil. (Note: I like to make sure all the anchor points are where I want them before I commit to finishing the ends.)

3 Form a diamond pattern inside the entire length of the snake's body with the 19-gauge wire by crossing the wires after they are anchored, and repeating the coiling technique approximately 2 inches (5.1 cm) above the last point on the opposite side. (Shorten these lengths near the end of the snake's body.) Continue until the tail is ¼ inch (6 mm) wide.

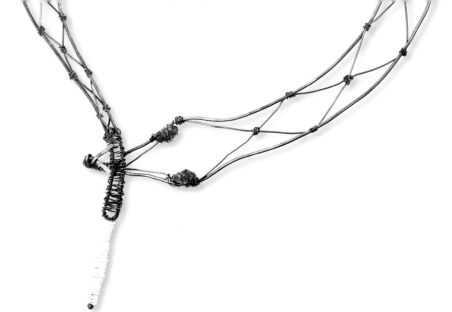

4 Finish the tail by wrapping both wires around the outline wires with a figure eight motion until the void is filled. Leave a 3-inch (7.6 cm) tail. Wind one side of the wire tail around the tip, clip it to ½ inch (1.3 cm), and hide the end.

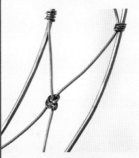

5 Confirm the anchor placements and finish each coil, hiding the ends. Anchor each wire intersection with the same coil technique. Lightly hammer the wrapped points of the diamond pattern to harden and secure the wire.

Finishing the Collar

1 Clean and finish the collar with wax. Add the graduated shell beads, largest to smallest, to the remaining tail wire. Secure the shell beads by bending a tiny coil with round-nose pliers.

2 Cut two pieces of 28-gauge steel wire, each 12 inches (30.5 cm) long. Center a crystal bead on each wire. (These are the snake's eyes.) Wrap each beaded wire around the widest points of the snake's head, encircling both the thick exterior and thin interior wires and the crystal bead.

3 I chose not to further shape the collar around the neck and shoulders for an Elizabethan Ruff effect. You may choose otherwise—simply put the final collar on a neck mandrel or form and carefully bend the collar around the shoulder with your hands or a mallet.

get teased about my relationship with the frozen-food delivery guy, who drives a burly yellow truck that delivers semi-prepared gourmet food. It's simple, it's minimal, it works for me. But some sassy friends have linked the naughty myth of the 50s milkman to my heroic driver-friend and nicknamed him John Don-Juan Schwan. The ikebana aspect is probably obvious—this piece's lovely aesthetic works for my eyes the way Schwan's works in my tummy!

JOHN DON-JUAN SCHWAN IKEBANA

Forming the Flower Motifs

1 Cut 24 inches (61 cm) of 19-gauge steel wire. Form a flower with five pointy petals, using the drawing as a guide. Secure the initial shape by wrapping the wire twice around the center of the flower. Form a second petal layer and secure it in the same way.

2 Cut a piece of 24-gauge steel wire, 36 inches (91.4 cm) long. Repeat the flower-making process from step 1. You will have a long wire tail remaining.

3 Hammer, clean, and finish both double-petaled wire flowers with wax.

Forming the Branch

1 Use a jeweler's saw to cut a 6-inch (15.2 cm) length of 9-gauge steel wire. Form it into a slight curve, then hammer and texture the wire into an organic branch form.

2 Choose one end of the wire to be the top of the branch. Mark a point that is 1¾ inches (4.4 cm) from the top. Use a center punch to divot the marked point, then drill a hole through the wire.

3 Clean the wire branch, and then finish it with wax.

Forming the Necklace

1 1. Cut a piece of 16-gauge steel wire 24 inches (61 cm) long. Using the drawing as a guide, form a leaf shape at one end of the wire. Make a perpendicular U-shaped bend in the wire just where the leaf shape ends. Hammer, clean, and wax the whole piece. Set this wire piece aside.

2 Nestle the two wire flowers together, with the larger flower on top. Insert their wire ends into the front of the hole drilled in the branch. Tightly secure the flowers in place by wrapping the wire several times.

3 At the center of the larger flower, create a focal area by adding the seed beads, in no particular order, to the longer tail. Continue binding the flowers onto the stem with the remaining wire.

4 Pin the flower/branch component on a necklace or dress form. Hook the leaf-shaped end of the 16-gauge wire piece around the bottom of the branch, 1 to 2 inches (2.5 to 5.1 cm) beneath the flower focal area. This forms the clasp of the neck ring.

5 Loop the remaining end of the 16-gauge wire around a necklace form and down to the flower-branch component, securing it with several twists. A tail should remain. As shown in the drawing, form a small leaf shape with this wire then clip off any excess. To finish the piece, wrap and tuck under the ends of the thinner wire.

MATERIALS & TOOLS

■ STEEL WIRE, 9, 16, 19, AND 24 GAUGE

■ VINTAGE SEED BEADS, GLASS AND STEEL

■ TOOL KIT, PAGE 27

■ CENTER PUNCH

■ FLEXIBLE SHAFT OR ELECTRIC DRILL

■ DRILL BIT, ⅟₁₆ INCH (1.6 MM)

■ NECKLACE FORM OR MANDREL

The snake said, "Sssssssss," to the Keeper of the Covey. "May I enter so my skin doesn't dry in the desert sun?" "Only if your intentions are pure. Eat not of the quail's eggs or your voice shall forever be immortalized in links of steel." The snake promised to abide peaceably within, only to devour the eggs when he gained entrance. The Keeper observed, "Trust a snake to be and do as only a snake can be and do." I designed this bracelet with S-shaped links—the actualization of my fable about character and truth.

SSSSSSSSS-LINK FABLE

MATERIALS & TOOLS

- **STEEL WIRE, 16 GAUGE**
- **3 VINTAGE KEYS**
- **TOOL KIT, PAGE 27**

AUTHOR'S NOTE

- ONCE CONNECTED, THE 13 LINKS IN THIS BRACELET MEASURE 7¼ INCHES (18.4 CM); ADJUST THE LENGTH OF YOUR PIECE ACCORDING TO YOUR WRIST AND CLASP SIZES.

Forming the S-Links

1 Cut 12 to 16 pieces of 16-gauge steel wire, each 2 inches (5.1 cm) long. File one end of each piece.

2 Grasp the filed tip of one wire with the widest part of round-nose pliers. Tightly bend the wire into a full circle with a complete turn of the pliers. Finish the S-link by repeating the action at the wire's other end.

3 Use flush cutters to remove any remaining wire. File the end if necessary, then hammer the link.

4 Repeat steps 2 and 3 for the rest of the wires cut in step 1.

5 Hold the loop of each link with flat- or bent-nose pliers. Move the pliers in opposite directions, using the center of the link as a pivot point.

Forming the Custom Toggle Clasp

1 Cut an 8-inch (20.3 cm) piece of 16-gauge steel wire.

2 Use pliers to form the wire into a custom shape that will fit around the largest vintage key and function as a secure clasp (see drawing). Twist the ends of the wire shape, finish with a wrapped loop, and file the wire's ends.

3 Make any necessary adjustments so that the keys fit through the toggle. Hammer the unit to work-harden it.

Assembling the Bracelet

1 Connect the links by fastening the loop of one link to the loop of another link as shown.

2 Connect the wrapped loop on the clasp to one end of the bracelet. Connect all of the keys to the last loop at the other end of the bracelet.

3 Clean the bracelet, and finish it with wax. (Keith LoBue's hand-wash cleaning method, described on page 26, works very well with this chain type.)

Ernestine, the switchboard operator in the hit 1970s TV-comedy *Laugh In*, counted rings until the "party to whom she was speaking" picked up. Fortunately she wasn't counting all the rings in this simple, but long (winded?) chain-mail belt! She would have surely ended up with a wrong number. Ring up your own funky psychedelic-meets-Medieval belt with ringy-dingies you make yourself!

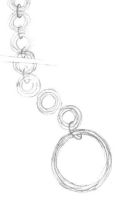

ONE RINGY-DINGY, TWO RINGY-DINGIES

MATERIALS & TOOLS

- STEEL WIRE, 16 GAUGE
- TOOL KIT, PAGE 27
- METAL RODS OR MANDRELS WITH THESE DIAMETERS:
  - ³⁄₁₆ INCH (5 MM)
  - ¼ INCH (6 MM)
  - ⁵⁄₁₆ INCH (8 MM)
  - ⁹⁄₁₆ INCH (14 MM)
- FORMING PLIERS (OPTIONAL)

Gauging the Belt's Length

1 Measure the circumference of your waist or hips where you plan to wear the belt. Add 3½ inches (8.9 cm) to the hip measurement. This extension will be the belt tail.

2 A 3-inch (7.6 cm) segment of the belt is made from six ³⁄₁₆-inch (5 mm) rings, three ¼-inch (6 mm) rings, three ⁵⁄₁₆-inch (8 mm) rings, and three ⁹⁄₁₆-inch (14 mm) rings. Determine how many segments you need to make your belt, how many rings of each size are required, and make these rings out of 16-gauge wire.

Assembling a Segment

1 Open a ⁵⁄₁₆-inch (8 mm) ring and close it around two ³⁄₁₆-inch (5 mm) rings.

2 Open a ⁹⁄₁₆-inch (14 mm) ring and close it around the two ³⁄₁₆-inch (5 mm) rings from the component made in step 1, pinching the ⁵⁄₁₆-inch (8 mm) ring out of the way. This forms a single segment.

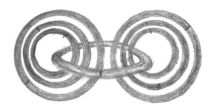

3 Repeat steps 1 and 2 to make as many single segments as necessary to form the belt and tail.

4 Connect two segments by opening a ¼-inch (6 mm) jump ring and closing it around the ³⁄₁₆-inch (5 mm) jump ring from two separate segments.

Forming the Focal Rings & Hook

1 Cut a 16-inch (40.6 cm) length of 16-gauge steel wire. Coil the wire around a 1⅛-inch (2.9 cm) mandrel at least three times. Cut the coils into large jump rings. Hammer the rings.

2 Cut 1¼-inches (3.2 cm) of 16-gauge steel wire. Bend a right angle ¼ inch (6 mm) from one end, then form a plain loop.

3 Bend the remaining section of the wire in half with the largest part of the round-nose pliers. Form a jaunty angle in the last ⅛ inch (3 mm), leaving a slight opening (see drawing). Hammer the hook.

Adding the Focal Rings & Hook

1 Attach the focal rings by fastening a ¼-inch (6 mm) jump ring around the three rings at one end of the belt.

2 Attach the hook by fastening a ¼-inch (6 mm) jump ring around the three rings at the opposite end of the belt and the hook.

3 Clean the belt and finish it with wax to seal.

AUTHOR'S NOTE

- YOU CAN BUY ALUMINUM ROD IN THE SIZES LISTED ABOVE FROM YOUR LOCAL HARDWARE STORE.

- STEEL WIRE, 12 AND 24 GAUGE
- GUN BLUEING
- GUN BROWNING
- TOOL KIT, PAGE 27
- SOLDERING TORCH
- STRIKER
- HEAT RESISTANT SOLDERING SURFACE (FIREBRICK)
- FLUX AND APPLICATOR
- SILVER SOLDER, EASY
- SNIPS
- SOLDER PICK
- TWEEZERS
- COPPER TONGS
- PICKLE IN WARMING POT
- SAFETY GLASSES AND FIRE EXTINGUISHER
- MANDREL, ½-INCH (1.3 CM) DIAMETER, OR RING MANDREL
- COTTON PADS AND RAGS

When nouns became verbs in this project, my universe started to tremble a bit. The answer to the question "Can steel wire be patinated?" came from a world far, far away from jewelry making—that of hunting and guns. I ended up with three subtle tones of steel chain: blue blackish (from blueing), brown plumish (from browning), and natural ironish (steel *au naturel!*).

BLUEING, BROWNING & IRON-ING

Preparing the Links

1 Cut 15 lengths of 12-gauge steel wire, each 4 inches (10.2 cm).

2 File the tips of the wires completely flat. Clean ½ inch (1.3 cm) of each wire end with fine steel wool.

Forming & Soldering the Chain Segments

1 Bend each end of one wire around a ½-inch (1.3 cm) mandrel. The bent wire should be oval in shape and its ends should butt together exactly.

2 Repeat step 1, adding the first link onto the new one before closing its ends. Continue this process to form a chain. Repeat with the remaining wires until you have three chains that are each five links long.

3 One at a time, place each five-link chain on a firebrick and solder each link closed with easy silver solder (see drawing). Pickle the chains, making sure to dry each one completely.

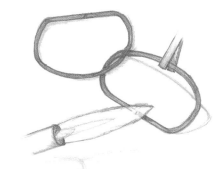

4 File off any remaining solder, and clean the chains with steel wool.

5 Hammer each link on all three chains into symmetrical ovals on a ring mandrel.

6 Hold both ends of each link with flat-nose pliers. Gently bend each link a quarter turn in opposite directions. This creates the traditional bend of curb chain.

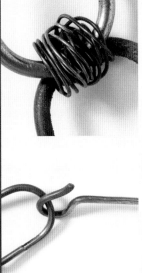

BLUEING, BROWNING & IRON-ING

Adding Patina to the Segments

① Following the manufacturer's directions, apply blueing solution with a cotton pad to one of the three sections of chain. Apply a layer of solution and wait until it dries. Repeat as desired to build up the desired depth of color.

② Following the process described above, apply browning solution to a different section of chain.

Creating the Hook Closure & Assembling the Necklace

① Cut two 24-inch (61 cm) lengths of 24-gauge steel wire. Lay an end link of the natural steel segment next to an end link of the browning link segment. Wrap one of the thin wires around the two links willy nilly. Hide the ends. Repeat to connect the browning and blueing link sections. Clean the wrapped links with a wire brush.

② Cut a 4½-inch (11.4 cm) length of 12-gauge steel wire. Bend a right angle 1¼ inches (3.2 cm) from one end and bend a plain loop with large round-nose pliers (see drawing, left side). Bend a right angle 1¾ inches (3.8 cm) from the opposite end and bend a hook shape and jaunty angle with the same round-nose pliers (see drawing, right side). Hammer and clean the hook.

③ Open and close the hook around the end link of the blueing link section. Finish the entire necklace with wax to seal.

Recent struggles with my cell phone have got me thinking that many everyday tools have become more complex and multi-purposed. Then again, the focal points in this bracelet—handmade to mimic clothespin spring links and a cotter pin closure—are quite the opposite. A cotter pin was used to hold a tiny wheel on an axle—simple and utilitarian. They reflect back on far simpler, more carefree days.

WHEN HARDWARE WAS EASY

Forming the Clothespin Links

1 Cut 10 pieces of 16-gauge wire, each 6 inches (15.2 cm) long. Set one wire piece aside.

2 Starting about one-third of the way from one wire end, and holding it at a slight angle to the mandrel, make a coil approximately ⅝-inch (1.6 cm) long; this should take four wraps. Keep all the wraps at the same slant. (Maintaining a consistent angle while making the coil will help the links move with ease.) End the coil so that the wire comes off the mandrel from the same side that the coil started.

3 Measure ⅞ inch (2.2 cm) down the wire from one end of the coil and mark this point. Measure and mark ⅞ inch (2.2 cm) from the other end of the coil. Form an inward right-angle bend at both marked points.

4 Trim each bent wire end so they meet at the center. File the ends and reshape the element.

5 Repeat steps 2 through 4 to form a total of nine links.

Forming the Connecting Link

1 Using the 6-inch (15.2 cm) wire length reserved in step 1, repeat step 2 under Forming the Clothespin Links.

2 Trim the excess wire at the ends of the coil to 1½ inches (3.8 cm) long. File the ends of the cut wire.

3 Using the midpoint of round-nose pliers, make a plain loop at each wire's end. The loops will curve in opposite directions to meet the straight wire (see drawing, A).

Forming the Cotter Pin Clasp

1 Cut 8 inches (20.3 cm) of 16-gauge steel wire. Loop the wire around the mandrel, making one-and-a-half turns and leaving a 2-inch (5.1 cm) extension at one end.

2 Following the drawing (B), form the remaining bends in the cotter pin. File the ends of the clasp.

MATERIALS & TOOLS

- **STEEL WIRE, 16 AND 28 GAUGE**
- **TOOL KIT, PAGE 27**
- **MANDREL, ⅛-INCH (3 MM) INNER DIAMETER**
- **LEATHER CORD, 1 MM ROUND**

AUTHOR'S NOTE

- THESE PROJECTS MAKE A 7¼-INCH (18.4 CM) BRACELET. ADJUST THE NUMBER OF LINKS TO FIT YOUR WRIST SIZE.

Assembling the Bracelet

1 To connect the bracelet links, hook the angled ends of each element into the coil of the adjacent link (drawing, C). Repeat this process until all the links have been used. Attach the connecting link with the looped ends to the last link.

2 Fit the loops from the connecting link around the last coil on the opposite side of the bracelet. Slip the straight side of the cotter pin through the newly joined coil. Clean and wax the bracelet.

3 Cut an 8-inch (15.2 cm) length of the leather cord. Double the cord and tie a Lark's head knot around the ring of the cotter pin. Thread both cords at the opposite end through one side of the last link's coil. Fold over ½ inch (1.3 cm).

4 Cut a 4-inch (10.2 cm) length of 28-gauge wire. Wind the wire tightly around the overlapped cording, snip the ends to ⅛ inch (3 mm), and hide them inside the coil.

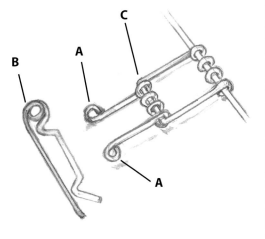

B   A   C   A   A

danced a little jig when I found the vintage chain (above) that inspired this design. The original stock was formed from stamped brass sheet metal. Though I liked the whimsical interplay of the links in the brass version, the hard part was getting my head around how to set up a jig to get the required consistency of size and shape for this design.

MATERIALS & TOOLS

- **STEEL WIRE, 16 GAUGE**
- **TOOL KIT, PAGE 27**
- **WOOD BLOCK MADE FROM FIVE-QUARTER DECKING BOARD, AT LEAST 5 INCHES (12.7 CM) WIDE**
- **2 DRILL BITS, ⁵⁄₁₆ INCH (8 MM) AND ¹⁷⁄₆₄ INCH (7 MM)**
- **2 HEX-HEAD LAG SCREWS, ⅜ X 1 INCH (1 X 2.5 CM) AND ⁵⁄₁₆ X 1 INCH (0.8 X 2.5 CM)**
- **RACHET WITH 13- AND 14-MM HEADS**

DANCE A LITTLE (HONEYCOMB) JIG

Creating the Jig

1 Drill two holes into the wood block, ⁵⁄₁₆ inch (8 mm) apart. (You may need to make pilot holes in the block so the wood doesn't split.)

2 Set the lag screws into the wood so that two straight sides of their heads are parallel (see drawing).

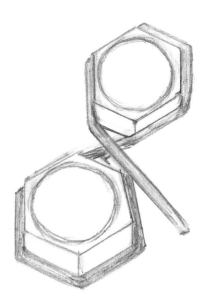

Forming the Links

1 Cut 41 pieces of 16-gauge steel wire, each 8 inches (20.3 cm) long. Set one wire aside.

2 Bend a right angle in one of the wire pieces, approximately 1½ inches (3.8 cm) from one end.

3 Set the angle in the wire alongside an angle in the smaller lag-screw head. Bend the tail around two more corners of the lag screw head to anchor the wire.

4 Span the space between the two lag-screw heads with the other end of the wire, and form it around each corner of the larger head. Take the wire back to the smaller head and form the wire all the way around it. Lift the link from the jig.

5 Cut the wire tail in the space between the two lag-screw heads. File the cut ends if necessary.

DANCE A LITTLE (HONEYCOMB) JIG

6 Hammer the figure-eight wire shape, and re-form it so that the links are nearly, but not quite, closed; exactitude isn't necessary. Set one link aside.

7 With the smaller loop at the bottom, hold a link so it looks like a backward S. Place the tip of the round-nose pliers in the link's middle. Use your fingers to fold the link in half over the pliers. Fold each link on a slant so that the smaller loop is in the front and further to the left than the larger loop (see drawing).

8 Repeat steps 2 through 7 to create a total of 39 folded links and one unfolded one.

Forming the Strands

1 Insert the smaller loop of one folded link through the larger loop of another. (Note: This may require lifting the wire ends a bit.) Join 18 folded links into a strand.

2 Repeat the linking process described in step 1 to form a separate strand with 21 folded links.

3 Lay out the strands, with the shorter one on top.

4 Make a ³⁄₁₆-inch (5 mm) steel wire jump ring. Attach the ring to the large end of the unfolded link and to *both* loops at one end of the shorter strand and one end of the longer strand.

Creating the Hook & Completing the Necklace

1 With the reserved piece of straight wire, form a large loop around the large lag-screw head on the jig. Form a right angle at the center point of the remaining straight section of wire.

2 Using the largest part of the jaws of round-nose pliers, bend a hook in the remaining wire and position it perpendicular to the larger loop.

3 Hammer the links, and attach the loop end of the hook to the unfinished ends of both strands.

4 File the links if necessary, then clean the piece and finish it with wax.

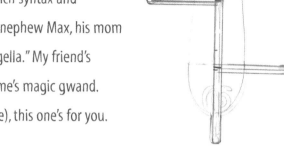

W e can learn a lot about language, in all its rich syntax and quirkiness, from children. According to my nephew Max, his mom apparently buys groceries at "piggella wiggella." My friend's three-year-old once misplaced her fairy-princess costume's magic gwand. To both these angels (and to clueless adults everywhere), this one's for you.

THE GWAND & SQUIGGELLA WIGGELLAS

Forming the Setting for the "Wand"

1 Cut 28 inches (71.1 cm) of 16-gauge steel wire. Form the wire using the drawing as a guide. Leave a tail of at least 3 inches (7.6 cm) at the top and create tabs and right-angle bends as you go. You'll end the shaping with the wire back at the starting point. Trim this end of the wire to the same length as that of the starting tail.

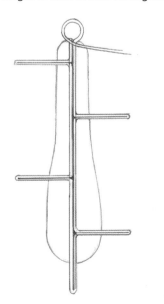

2 Hammer and clean the shaped wire, but not the tails at the top of the form.

3 Cut four pieces of 19-gauge wire, each 6 inches (15.2 cm) long. As shown in the detail photos, use one wire to bind each of the four tabs to the spine. Lightly hammer the structure and clean the connections.

4 Form a large loop from each tail wire, curving one in one direction and the other in the opposite direction. Wrap the ends of the wire around the stem of the loop. Closely trim the ends. Hammer and clean the loops. Wax the entire setting.

5 Use round-nose pliers to bend the bottom-most left and right tabs of the setting to fit over the oval stone. This will take a bit of finessing and several adjustments and rechecks to get the fit right.

6 Fit the oval stone into the open end of the "wand," the found metal vessel. (I removed the dried sponge tip from my vintage envelope moistener.)

- STEEL WIRE, 16 AND 19 GAUGE
- CIGAR-SHAPED FOUND METAL VESSEL WITH ONE OPEN END (PROJECT FEATURES A VINTAGE ENVELOPE MOISTENER)
- OVAL STONE TO FIT OPEN END OF THE VESSEL
- TOOL KIT, PAGE 27
- MANDREL, ¼ INCH (6 MM)

Forming the Squiggly Necklace

❶ Cut lengths of 16-gauge steel wire to the following measurements:

- two pieces, each 10 inches (25.4 cm)
- two pieces, each 9 inches (22.9 cm)
- two pieces, each 8 inches (20.3 cm)
- two pieces, each 7 inches (17.8 cm)
- two pieces, each 6 inches (15.2 cm)
- two pieces, each 5 inches (12.7 cm)
- one piece, 4 inches (10.2 cm)

❷ As shown in the drawing, use round-nose pliers and your fingers to form the wires into squiggly, spiraling links. End each link with a plain loop. Note: Be sure to form the 4-inch (10.2 cm) wire squiggle with ample room to hold a ⅝-inch (1.6 cm) jump ring inside the spiral. Hammer the spiral links to harden and flatten them.

❸ Form 17 jump rings from 16-gauge wire, each with an inner diameter of ¼ inch (6 mm). Hammer the jump rings.

❹ Attach two pairs of jump rings to the pair of loops at the top of the setting.

❺ Lay out the necklace components, placing six squiggly links on each side of the pendant. Position the largest links nearest the pendant and gradually decrease the size of the links on both sides of the necklace. Connect the links with jump rings, feeding one ring through the loop of one link and through the adjacent link's outer spiral.

❻ Finish one end of the necklace with the 4-inch (10.2 cm) link and the other with an extra jump ring to use as the clasp. Clean and wax the necklace.

W hen beauty and utility must converge, designers can really test their mettle. This custom-formed bail works a bit like a pair of utilitarian tongs that seems to have tweezed a specimen up from its cozy earthen bed. Besides working as an intriguing display, the bail offers a peek to the flip side of this archaeological wonder.

TONGS BAIL

1 Cut 12 inches (30.5 cm) of 16-gauge steel wire. With forming pliers or a mandrel, form a ring at the center of the wire, ending the circle with the wire's tail ends crossing each other.

2 Holding the ring stable with pliers, use a pair of pliers with serrated jaws to twist together both wire tails under the ring. One full turn is all you need to hold the connection, but more turns will offer embellishment.

3 Adjust the tails of the wire so they are slightly wider than the object to be held. Bend the end of one tail to fit inside a drilled hole, allowing approximately ¼ inch (6 mm) for clearance (see drawing). Repeat this process with the second tail on the other side of the object to be held.

4 Hammer the bail, holding the wire in place at the desired angle. Clean the wire, and finish it with wax.

5 String the pendant on the black cotton cord or make an adjustable knot closure (see below).

VARIATION: MAKING AN ADJUSTABLE KNOT CLOSURE

1 Cut the waxed cotton cord in half, and tie each piece to the ⁷⁄₁₆-inch (1.1 cm) ring.

2 Tie a loose knot approximately ½ inch (1.3 cm) from the end of one of the loose cords.

3 Pass the other piece of cord through the knot and tighten it. Knot the remaining loose end onto the cord, more or less opposite the first knot.

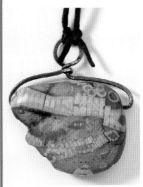

A caged stone gathers no moss. (Mixed metaphors can be as fun as mixed materials if you play it right.) Take your pick of a Leland Blue cabochon (plucked from the shores of Lake Michigan, where smelting factories dumped this ore byproduct), a toy billiard ball, or a plain ole rock, plus wound-tight-as-a-clock steel wire.

CAGED STONE

Forming the Caged Pendant

1 Wrap the rock, fossil, or cabochon in the half-sheet of tissue paper. On the paper, mark the position of the top of the object.

2 Cut 40 inches (1 m) of 19-gauge steel wire. At a point 4 inches (10.2 cm) from one end of the wire, bend a right angle.

3 Lay the right angle of the wire at the top of the object. Tightly wrap the wire, in a haphazard fashion, around the tissue-wrapped stone, leaving a tail 2 inches (5.1 cm) long. The tail should end on the side opposite the point where the wrapping began.

4 With the 2-inch (5.1 cm) tail, form a loop atop a short neck (see drawing). Cut off any excess wire. Randomly wrap the 4-inch (10.2 cm) tail around the neck. Tuck in the wire end with pliers.

5 Remove the tissue paper with tweezers or pliers and clean the wire. Orient the loop so it's perpendicular to the face of the stone.

Embellishing with Barbs (Optional)

In addition to being decorative, this process is useful if the wire wraps need to be stabilized in any areas.

1 Cut five to eight pieces of 28-gauge wire, each 3 inches (7.6 cm) long. At the center of each wire, make a U-shaped bend.

2 Position the U-shaped wires at the intersection of two or three of the wires wrapped around the object, and tightly wrap the tails several times. Clip the ends to form miniature wire barbs. Tuck the ends close for a less "prickly" version. File all of the ends smooth.

Forming the Neck Ring

1 Cut a piece of 16-gauge steel wire that is 24 inches (61 cm) long. At the center of the wire, bend a tight U-shaped divot approximately ½-inch (1.3 cm) deep.

2 Shape the rest of the wire into a neck ring approximately 6 or 7 inches (15.2 or 17.8 cm) in diameter. The wire ends will overlap at the back. Form a U-shaped hook at each end of the neck wire. Turn one hook perpendicular to the other.

3 File and forge the wire ends, hammer the neck ring, clean it, and finish it with wax.

4 Using a rubber or rawhide mallet if necessary, bend the wire neck ring over a dress form or neck mandrel to give it a gentle curve.

5 Add the cage pendant to the neck ring, resting the pendant's bail in the divot.

- STEEL WIRE, 16, 19, AND 28 GAUGE
- ROCK, FOSSIL, OR CABOCHON
- TISSUE PAPER, HALF SHEET
- TOOL KIT, PAGE 27
- TWEEZERS (OPTIONAL)
- DRESS FORM OR NECKLACE MANDREL

Far from the math-y, science-y, statistics-y bell curve stuff, the Ball Curve is more, um, (well) artsy fartsy. The traditional bell curve is a visually informative plot of the distribution of a given data set. The Ball Curve, on the other hand, is steel wire arched to fit a No. 10 Ball canning lid. The lid is held by tabs and suspended by loops, so a bit of engineering snuck into the equation after all. Now, isn't that what our science teachers told us? That this stuff would be important some day?

MATERIALS & TOOLS

- **STEEL WIRE, 16 AND 19 GAUGE**
- **VINTAGE GLASS CANNING LID**
- **RIBBON OF YOUR CHOICE, 20 INCHES (51 CM), PROJECT FEATURES A RICH GRAY VELVET**
- **TOOL KIT, PAGE 27**
- **WHITE CHALK PENCIL OR CORRECTION FLUID**
- **RIBBON "MANDREL" OF SHEET METAL OR HEAVY CARDBOARD, ½ INCH (1.3 CM)**

THE BALL CURVE

Forming the Setting

1. Cut a piece of 16-gauge steel wire, 30 inches (76.2 cm) long.

2. Create a small plain loop at one end of the wire with round-nose pliers. Starting at the 3-o'clock position and working clockwise around the template, form the wire into the tabs and loops shown in the drawing. As soon as each tab is formed, use two pair of pliers to create the prongs: one to hold it flat and one to pinch the gap closed. Check the wire armature against the glass lid for correct fit as you go.

3. Cut a wire tail to ½ inch (1.3 cm) past the initial loop as indicated in the drawing, guide the end of the wire through the loop, and file the wire's end. Turn the tail to make a securing loop around the first loop.

4. Hammer, clean, and wax the wire setting.

Fitting & Securing the Setting

1. Secure the lid snugly in the setting.

2. Fit the setting over the back of the glass lid and carefully mark the wire ¹⁄₁₆ inch (1.6 mm) past the lid edge with a white pencil or correction fluid. Remove the lid and bend right angles with two pliers to make a crisp bend directly at these points. Replace the lid and check the fit.

3. Again mark the wire ¹⁄₁₆ inch (1.6 mm) above the lid edge. Remove the lid and bend crisp right angles at these points.

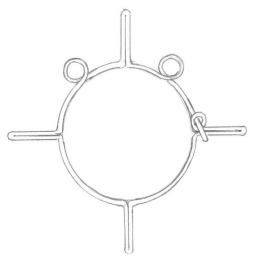

THE BALL CURVE

④ Open each of the four "prongs" slightly at their base, replace the lid, and check the fit once again. When all the prongs fit correctly, bend each entire prong back inward (see drawing). Adjust each bend slightly, working around the setting two or three times.

Creating the Connectors & Hooks

① Cut two pieces of 19-gauge wire, each 12 inches (30.5 cm) long. Wind one of the wires around the ribbon mandrel, reserving the last 2 inches (5.1 cm) of wire. Form a wrapped loop with the reserved wire as shown in the drawing. Closely file both ends of the wire and tuck them in. Repeat this process to make a second connector. Clean and wax each connector.

② Thread one end of the ribbon down through the wire connector, around the bottom "rung," then back up to the top. Holding the ribbon in place, hammer the connector tight and flat against the ribbon. (The "rungs" of the connector will slant as they are flattened.)

③ Repeat step 2 at the other end of the ribbon, making sure the wrapped loops are on the same side.

④ Cut two lengths of 19-gauge wire, each 3 inches (7.6 cm) long. Double the wire using the pinching technique (Forming the Setting, page 89, step 2). Bend a hook at the doubled end at the 1-inch (2.5 cm) mark and bend a plain loop ½ inch (1.3 cm) from the opposite end.

⑤ Clean and wax each hook.

Assembling the Necklace

① Open and close one of the loops of a hook around a wrapped loop of the ribbon connector. Repeat to the opposite end, adding on the hooks in the same direction.

② Hook the hooks to the loop "ears" on the setting. These will serve as the clasp/closure.

A symbol of potential (as well as a lot of other things), the lotus flower is steeped in meaning. It emerges from watery depths to open during the day then recedes again at night. The rustic prong setting on this ring mimics the flower; its soft silver-gray cradle coddles a treasure from the deep (South)—a Civil War–era marble. Use my design to let just about any plain, odd little memento reach its full promise!

YA GOT POTENTIAL, KID

Creating the Pattern

1 Estimate the size of the pattern by first measuring the circumference of your object. Subtract a minimum of ¼ inch (6 mm) from that figure. Select a circle-drawing template that matches this measurement. For example, my marble measured 2¼ inches (5.7 cm), so I used the 2-inch (5.1 cm) circle on the template.

2 With a pencil, mark the quarter points on the circle. Draw petals connecting each quarter point to the center.

Forming the Ring's Foundation

1 Cut a 24-inch (60.9 cm) length of 16-gauge wire. Bend a right angle to the first ⅜ inch (1 cm) of one end. Positioning the short tail at the flower center, start forming the wire at the center of the circle, and work the 16-gauge wire to the top of the prong. Mark this point with a white chalk pencil or correction fluid. With the mark remaining at the tip of the prong, use the tip of round-nose pliers to bend a soft U-shaped turn in the wire.

2 Work the wire back down to the center of the circle and mark this turning point for the next bend. Wrap the wire around the short tail.

3 Repeat steps 1 and 2 to finish bending the wire and complete the pattern (see drawing). Hammer and texture the outside of the flower with a leather or other texture stamp.

MATERIALS & TOOLS

- STEEL WIRE, 16 GAUGE
- MARBLE OR OTHER FOUND OBJECT
- TOOL KIT, PAGE 27
- PAPER, PENCIL, TAPE MEASURE, AND CIRCLE-DRAWING TEMPLATE
- WHITE CHALK PENCIL OR CORRECTION FLUID
- FORMING PLIERS (OPTIONAL)
- LEATHER OR OTHER TEXTURE STAMP

Creating the Band & Finishing the Ring

1 Hammer the remainder of the wire length. Place the flower (neck first) on top of a ring mandrel at the desired ring size.

2 Wrap the wire flatly around this point twice, and then up and around the neck of the flower several times tightly (see drawing). Trim any excess wire and tuck in the end with crimping or other pliers.

3 Clean the ring and seal with wax.

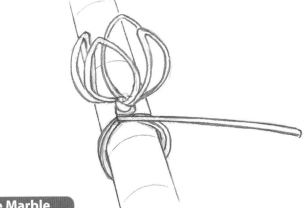

Setting the Marble

1 One at a time, bend each prong petal incrementally upward with forming or large round-nose pliers, checking the fit around the marble after each round of bends. Take care to bend the prongs similarly and evenly. (Since this design works with one continuous wire length, each move to a prong will affect the others.)

2 Bend the petal prongs close enough to secure a marble, but apart enough so the marbles may be interchanged, if desired. Add the marble to the setting.

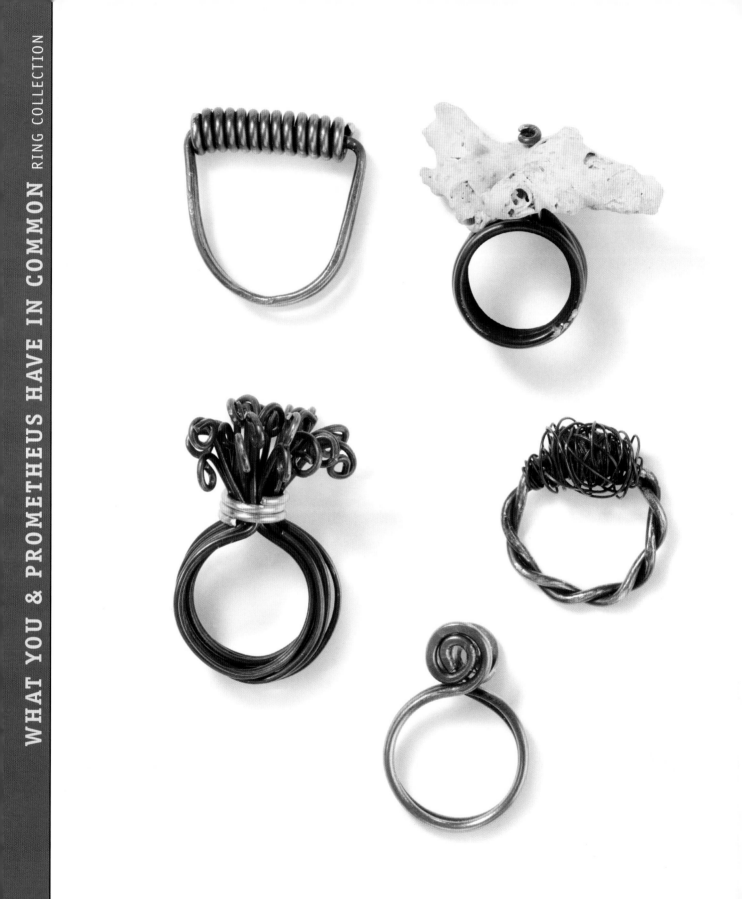

Prometheus didn't get to choose from a set of six iron rings for his desolate fate in Greece; likely he didn't want his famed iron rings at all. Poor (Titan) guy's final punishment from the big dog Zeus was to wear a band fashioned from the chain that bound him to Caucasus, set with a chip from the mountain itself as a reminder of his earlier offenses (having to do with fire, meat, and um, all of mankind).

MATERIALS & TOOLS FOR DOUBLE CURLY!

- STEEL WIRE, 16 GAUGE
- TOOL KIT, PAGE 27
- RING MANDREL

DOUBLE CURLY!

Step by Step

1 Cut a 7-inch-long (17.8 cm) piece of 16-gauge steel wire. Center the wire on a ring mandrel at the desired size. Tightly wrap the wire one and one-half times around the mandrel.

2 At each wire end, use round-nose pliers to form a spiral (see drawing). Center the spirals at the top of the ring.

3 Hammer the wire spirals, clean the ring, and finish it with wax.

TWIST & SLUB

Step by Step

1 Cut two pieces of 16-gauge steel wire, each 6 inches (15.2 cm) long. Hold both pieces together. Tighten one end of the pair in the vise and the other end in the chuck of the drill.

2 To twist the wire, slowly run the drill until the desired degree of twist is achieved. Loosen and remove the twisted wire from the vise and drill.

3 Center the twisted wire on a ring mandrel at the desired size. Completely wrap the wire around the mandrel, bypassing the ends (see drawing). Remove the wire from the mandrel and trim the ends so they overlap by ¼ inch (6 mm) or less.

4 Place the ring in a lined vise with the overlapped area centered and upright. Tighten the vise.

MATERIALS & TOOLS FOR TWIST & SLUB

- STEEL WIRE, 16 AND 28 GAUGE
- TOOL KIT, PAGE 27
- RING MANDREL
- VISE

TWIST & SLUB

5 Cut a piece of 28-gauge steel wire that is 36 inches (91.4 cm) long. To create the slub focal feature, tightly bind the ring where the band wires overlap. Trim and hide the wire ends.

6 Hammer only the band, avoiding the slub. Clean the ring and finish it with wax.

CORRALLED CORAL

Step by Step

1 Cut a piece of 16-gauge wire 20 inches (50.8 cm) long. Cut a piece of 19-gauge wire 4 inches (10.2 cm) long.

2 Coil one end of the 19-gauge wire around the 16-gauge wire loosely enough so that the bound wire can slide the length of the thicker wire.

3 With a short tail to start, wrap the 16-gauge wire seven times around the ring mandrel, centering the 19-gauge component as you go. Cut the ends, leaving an additional ⅜- to ½ inch (1 to 1.2 cm) at each end. File the ends, clean the piece, and finish it with wax.

4 As shown in the drawing, feed the drilled coral piece onto the 19-gauge wire and slide it close to the wrapped band.

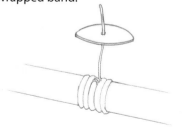

5 Trim the 19-gauge wire so it extends ⅜ inch (1 mm) past the coral. With the smallest part of round-nose pliers, form a tight coil in the thin wire to secure the coral.

DOUBLE-BANDED COIL

Step by Step

1 Cut a piece of 16-gauge wire 12 inches (30.5 cm) long. Cut two additional pieces, each 3½ inches (8.9 cm) long.

2 Coil the 12-inch (30.5 cm) wire around the ³⁄₁₆-inch (8 mm) mandrel. Trim the ends to form a 1-inch-long (2.5 cm) coil. File the wire ends.

3 Align the pair of 3½-inch (8.9 cm) wires. Bend a right angle at one end of each wire. Hammer each wire.

4 Fit the angled ends of both wires into one end of the coil. Wrap the remaining wire around a ring mandrel at the desired size (see drawing). Bend a right angle at the opposite ends of the wire so the double band will fit into the other end of the coil.

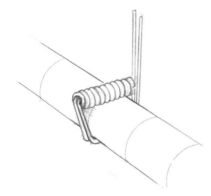

5 Hammer the wire ends into the coil, and hammer the band against the ring mandrel. Clean the ring and finish it with wax.

FIDDLEHEADS

Step by Step

1 Cut a piece of the 16-gauge brass wire 6 inches (15.2 cm) long. Tightly wrap the wire around the ¼-inch (6 mm) mandrel three times. Trim and file the wire ends and set the coil aside.

2 Cut 10 pieces of 19-gauge steel wire, each 5 inches (12.7 cm) long.

3 Align the lengths of steel wire and tightly bind them in the center with 28-gauge wire or a twist tie.

4 Bend the wire bundle around the ring mandrel at the desired size, overlapping its ends at the center top. Bend right angles in each wire end with flat-nosed pliers.

5 Fit the brass coil over the ends of the wire bundle and down to the apex of the ring band. Clip off the thin binding wire or twist tie.

6 Starting from the outside and working toward the center, use needle-nose pliers to bend tiny teardrop shapes in each wire end.

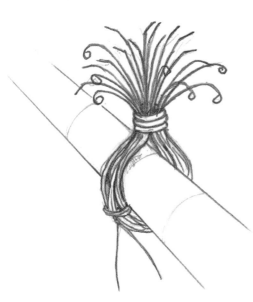

7 Fit the ring back on the ring mandrel and hammer the band. Clean the ring and finish it with wax.

MATERIALS & TOOLS FOR DOUBLE-BANDED COIL

- STEEL WIRE, 16 GAUGE
- TOOL KIT, PAGE 27
- MANDREL, 3⁄16 INCH (8 MM)
- RING MANDREL

MATERIALS & TOOLS FOR FIDDLEHEADS

- BRASS WIRE, 16 GAUGE
- STEEL WIRE, 19 GAUGE
- STEEL WIRE, 28 GAUGE OR A TWIST TIE
- TOOL KIT, PAGE 27
- MANDREL, ¼ INCH (6 MM)
- RING MANDREL

thought I was the belle of the State Fair Ball with the name necklace made especially for me. Decades before, famed sculptor and jeweler Alexander Calder created a name cuff for his wife, Louisa. He went on to create many such pieces for family, friends, and followers. I wonder, though, if even Calder was first at this name game. Might early peoples have made such adornments from carved bone, bent saplings, or fur? Here's your chance to express your own fabulousness—in steel wire.

- STEEL WIRE, 16, 19,
  AND 24 GAUGE
- TOOL KIT, PAGE 27
- GRAPH PAPER AND PENCIL

WHAT'S IN A NAME?

Forming the Pendant

1 Mark off an area of the graph paper with the intended size of your pendant. Draw the name inside it. Use your own handwriting or mimic a favorite font. Plan the connection points for the necklace. (I used the top loop of the "C" and the flourish of the "e.")

2 Cut a piece of 16-gauge steel wire long enough to "write" the name. It took approximately 40 inches (1 m) for this large-scale name.

3 Working left to right, form the wire to the shape of the name in your template.

Tips

• Close up any U-shaped curves.

• Create the tip of an R by forming a closed U-shaped curve toward the back of the pendant, then twisting it to the side and forming a right angle to form the top ledge.

• Add extended flourishes to the first and last letters.

4 Cut 2-inch (5.1 cm) lengths of 19- or 24-gauge steel wire and bind the name wherever reinforcement is needed, but especially wherever any wires overlap.

5 File the wire ends. Forge the ends of the first and last letters. Turn a backward-facing plain loop at the end of the last letter.

6 Bend all of the letters together, at the same time, into a gentle upward curve. Hammer the name, then clean it.

Forming the Barbell Links

1 Cut 20 pieces of 19-gauge steel wire, each 1½ inches (3.8 cm) long. File both ends of each piece.

2 Using the mid-point of round-nose pliers, form plain loops at each end of the wire (see drawing). Hammer the necklace links.

WHAT'S IN A NAME?

Forming the Clasp Links

1 Cut a piece of 19-gauge steel wire, 2 inches (5.1 cm) long. Using the mid-point of round-nose pliers, form a plain loop at one end. With the largest part of the pliers, form a larger plain loop at the other end (see drawing).

2 Cut a piece of 19-gauge steel wire, 2½ inches (6.4 cm) long. Use the mid-point of round-nose pliers to form a plain loop at one end. Use the largest part of the pliers to form a larger, not-quite-closed plain loop at the other end. Give the end of the loop a jaunty angle to make it a hook (see drawing, top right).

3 Hammer the clasp links.

Assembling the Necklace

1 Join the barbell links by their loops, placing one clasp link at each end of the chain.

2 Attach the looped clasp at one end of the chain around the loop of the first letter of the pendant. Attach the hook at the opposite end of the chain around the loop of the last letter.

3 Clean and wax the necklace.

This sea-worn shard of Mexican pottery and Gulliver the traveler have at least two things in common: They have both washed up on distant shores and have been tied down Lilliputian-style. The pottery shard may not have had as much travel-drama before my boys found it on the beach in Cozumel (I got the pick of the booty by enacting the Mom Tax), but you never know. Now here's a new kind of classic!

GULLIVER & THE LILLIPUTIANS

Forming the Frame for the Shard

1 Cut a piece of 12-gauge wire, 18 inches (45.7 cm) long.

2 Place your shard or found object on a piece of paper and trace closely around it to create a template.

3 Form the 18-inch (45.7 cm) wire piece around the bottom and sides of the template, leaving a ¹⁄₁₆-inch (1.6 mm) gap between the shard and the wire. Hammer the wire to flatten and texture it.

4 To finish the top of the frame, overlap the ends of the wire, and then trim them so they extend beyond the shard's widest point by ¼ to ½ inch (6 to 13 mm). Hammer the wire to flatten and texture it.

5 Drill a hole at the point where the wires overlap and also at each end of the wire.

Forming the Frames for the Dentelles

1 Cut two pieces of 12-gauge steel wire, each 4 inches (10.2 cm) long.

2 Place your dentelles on a piece of paper and trace closely around them to create a template.

3 Form each wire piece around the bottom and sides of the templates, leaving a ¹⁄₁₆-inch (1.6 mm) gap between each dentelle and wire. Hammer the wires to flatten and texture them.

4 Overlap the ends of the wires, and then trim them so they extend beyond the dentelle's widest point by ¼ to ½ inch (6 to 13 mm). Hammer the wires to flatten and texture them.

5 Cut two pieces of 19-gauge steel wire, each 2 inches (5.1 cm) long. As shown in the drawing, wrap one around each round frame several times at the point where the thick wire overlaps itself.

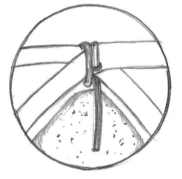

6 Trim, file, and hide the ends of the 19-gauge wires. Clean the round frames with fine wool.

MATERIALS & TOOLS

- **STEEL WIRE, 12 AND 19 GAUGE**
- **POTTERY SHARD OR SIMILAR FOUND OBJECT, 1¼ X 3 X ¼ INCH (3.2 X 7.6 X 0.6 CM)**
- **2 VINTAGE IVORY DENTELLES**
- **TOOL KIT, PAGE 27**
- **TITANIUM DRILL BIT, ¹⁄₁₆ INCH (1.5 MM)**

Securing the Shard

1 Cut a piece of 19-gauge steel wire, 20 inches (50.8 cm) long.

2 Wrap one end of the wire two or three times around an upper corner of the shard's frame (drawing, A). Position the shard within the frame. Pull the wire across the front of the shard to the other side of the frame. Wrap the thin wire around this side of the frame several times (drawing, B).

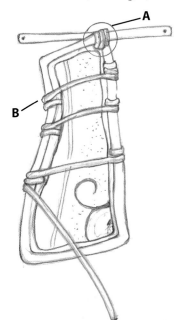

3 Pull the wire across the back of the shard to the other side of the frame. Wrap the thin wire around this side of the frame several times. Repeat this sequence (steps 2 and 3) until the shard is securely set in the frame. Trim, file, and hide the wire's ends.

4 Straighten any kinks in the 19-gauge wire, and press the wraps flat to the bezel with flat-nose pliers. Slide a thin piece of plastic between the shard and the wire. Clean the piece, and finish the metal with wax.

Securing the Dentelles

1 Cut six pieces of 19-gauge steel wire, each 3 inches (7.6 cm) long, to use as prongs. Set three of these pieces aside.

2 Measure, mark, and drill six evenly spaced holes around each round dentelle frame.

GULLIVER & THE LILLIPUTIANS

3 Measure ¼ inch (6 mm) in from one end of a 3-inch (7.6 cm) wire length. Using flat-nose pliers, bend a right angle at this point.

4 From the back of the frame, fit one wire's bent end into a drilled hole. Bend an angle in the wire at the apex of the dentelle, and then fit the wire into a hole on the opposite side of the frame.

5 Repeat steps 3 and 4 twice, using the remaining 3-inch (7.6 cm) wires as shown in the drawing.

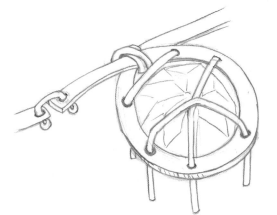

6 Trim each prong to ½ inch (1.3 cm), then flatten it with a hammer. Clean the prongs, and seal them with wax.

7 Insert a dentelle and roughly bend each prong into position (see drawing, top right, A). Gradually move each prong into place to achieve a close and secure fit (drawing B).

Forming the Clasp & Assembling the Necklace

1 Cut two pieces of 12-gauge wire, each 7 inches (17.8 cm) long. Form a plain loop at one end of one wire, and forge the end flat. Form a hook at one end of the second wire piece.

2 Bend both wires into slight curves, and hammer them flat. Drill a centered hole through the plain end of each wire.

3 Arrange all of the necklace components for assembly.

4 Cut six ½-inch (1.3 cm) pieces of 19-gauge steel wire to use as connectors. Link the components with these wires by forming tiny loops with round-nose pliers (top right drawing, C). The outer holes in the dentelle frames should overlap and match up with the holes in the plain ends of the clasp segments.

5 Clean the newly formed pieces, and finish with wax.

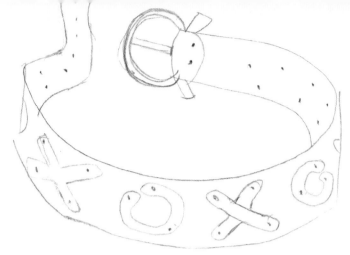

My son's lovebird suffers from unrequited love. You see, Earl (Earlybird for long) is a singlet. A mate-less bird tends to get attached to his keeper, but Earl has found a lovelier partner in his little dangle-mirror. He has found love—the unrequited kind. This belt's infinite circle of Xs and Os is dedicated to Earl. That's a lotta love for such a little peach head!

UNREQUITED LOVE

Forming & Attaching the Motifs

1 Cut eight pieces of 12-gauge steel wire, each 4 inches (10.2 cm) long. Cut 16 pieces of 12-gauge steel wire, each 1¾ inches (4.4 cm) long.

2 Bend the 4-inch (10.2 cm) wires around the 1⅛-inch (2.9 cm) mandrel to form the O motifs. Trim the overlapping wire and file the ends. Hammer, clean, and seal the wires.

3 Hammer the 1¾-inch (4.4 cm) wire pieces. File the ends then clean and seal the wires. These will be used to form the X motifs.

4 Using a center punch or awl, punch three divots in the wire Os—one near each end of the wire and one directly across the circle. Punch a divot near each end of all the Xs (see drawing). Drill through the divots, and file away any burrs.

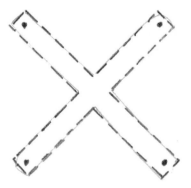

5 Evenly arrange the motifs on the belt between the snaps and the buckle tongue. Using the holes drilled in the motifs as guides, drill holes through the belt.

6 Cut 32 pieces of the waxed linen and use the needle to sew the wire X and O motifs onto the belt.

- STEEL WIRE, 9, 12, AND 16 GAUGE
- WORN OR RECYCLED BELT WITH SNAP BUCKLE OPENING
- IRISH WAXED LINEN, 4 PLY OR HEAVIER
- TOOL KIT, PAGE 27
- MANDRELS, 1⅛ INCHES (2.9 CM) AND 2¼ INCHES (5.7 CM)
- CENTER PUNCH OR AWL
- TITANIUM BIT, 1⁄16 INCH (1.6 MM)
- NEEDLE, TO FIT THROUGH DRILLED HOLE

Forming & Attaching the Buckle

1 Cut a piece of 9-gauge steel wire, 7 inches (17.8 cm) long.

2 Following the drawing below, form the wire three-quarters of the way around a 2¼-inch (5.7 cm) mandrel. Form right angles at each end with the remaining wire, continuing to forge, shape, and harden. Hammer the wire until it measures 1⁄16 inch (1.6 mm) thick. Clean the wire and seal it with wax.

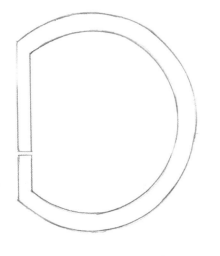

3 Cut a piece of 16-gauge steel wire, 3½ inches (8.9 cm) long, to use as the buckle's tongue. On one end of this wire, form a plain loop that fits around the straight side of the buckle (see drawing). The tongue must be long enough to lie across the buckle opening plus ¼ inch (6 mm). File the end of the tongue.

4 Hammer, clean, and seal the tongue. Attach it to the back of the buckle. Feed the steel buckle onto the leather belt and snap it closed.

MATERIALS & TOOLS

- **STEEL WIRE, 16 GAUGE**
- **WAXED COTTON CORD, BLACK, 2 MM, 24 INCHES (60 CM)**
- **WAXED HEMP TWINE, GREEN, 20 POUND (9 K) TEST, 9 FEET (2.7 M)**
- **TOOL KIT, PAGE 27**
- **BEADER'S GLUE**

His wife Louisa aside, Calder's greatest muse was, quite simply, the world around him. His jewelry embraces the tribal aesthetic, incorporating the natural marks left by hammer strikes and his intentions. The encouragement of what he called the "primitive and vigorous" over technique and flourish is the reason so many studio jewelers have been drawn to his work, and it is this core connection that unites one soul to another.

ZULU IN TEAL

Creating the Pins

1 Cut 25 pieces of 16-gauge steel wire:
  - ten 6-inch (15.2 cm) lengths
  - ten 7-inch (17.8 cm) lengths
  - five 8-inch (20.3 cm) lengths

2 Using round-nose pliers, form a U-shaped curve in the center of one of the wires. Continue shaping the wire to form a safety-pin-style loop. Repeat this step with the other wires.

3 Hammer the wires and clean them.

Forming the Coil & Peg Clasp

1 Cut a piece of 16-gauge steel wire, 1½ inches (3.8 cm) long. Form a plain loop at one wire end. File the other wire end. Hammer and clean the wire. This is the peg part of the clasp.

2 Cut a piece of 16-gauge steel wire, 12 inches (30.5 cm) long. Wrap the wire around a hardened piece of 16-gauge wire scrap about 15 times, creating a 1-inch (2.5 cm) coil. Form a plain loop in the remaining wire.

3 Slightly bend the coil into a gentle curve. Hammer the loop on the coil. Clean the entire component.

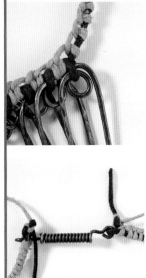

Assembling the Necklace

1 Group the wire pins by size: long, medium, and short.

2 Thread one of the long pins onto the center of the waxed cotton cord and tie an overhand knot around the wire loop. Tie two more long pins on one side of the first pin, leaving 4- to 5-mm spaces between them (see drawing). Using the same spacing, tie the remaining long pins on the other side of the center pin.

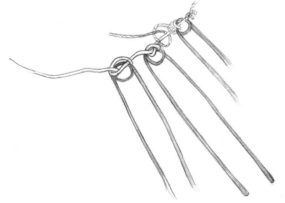

3 Tie the medium pins onto the waxed cotton cord, five on each side of the long pins and evenly spaced.

4 Tie the short pins onto the waxed cotton cord, five on each side of the medium pins and evenly spaced.

5 Use overhand knots to tie one half of the coil-and-peg clasp to each end of the cord, leaving 1¼-inch-long (3.2 cm) tails.

6 Slightly loosen the knot on one part of the clasp and insert one end of the waxed hemp. Retighten the knot.

7 Using the waxed hemp, closely and evenly hand-tie a series of blanket or half-hitch stitches down the cotton cord until you reach the first short pin.

8 Continue to hand-tie the hemp, making two stitches between each pin, until you reach the last short pin. Stitch the remainder of the cord. Loosen the final knot and insert the end of the hemp. Retighten the knot.

9 Wax the entire necklace, cord and twine included. Dot the clasp knots with cyanoacrylate glue.

I like to think of a time when official Namers assigned monikers to things they saw or experienced for the first time, and doing so with solemn head-nods and flourishing gestures of their sparkly gold scepters. But they missed with butterflies, because they don't resemble butter at all (they'd never live through the first hot summer day). Those Namers ought to have called me. I hereby pronounce them Japanese-candy-paper-for-wings flies.

BUTTER(REALLY?)FLY

Creating & Decorating the Butterfly Wings

1 Cut a 24-inch (60.9 cm) length of 19-gauge steel wire. Bend a right angle at the 2-inch (5.1 cm) mark and continue to bend the wire, using the drawing as a template. Bind the middle of the wings.

2 Hammer and clean the wing component.

3 Trace the butterfly wings onto Japanese candy paper. Cut the paper slightly larger than each wing.

4 Arrange the component so that the wings are elevated, level, and on the same plain, several inches above your wax paper work surface. (Use the wire tail as a prop and stand.)

5 Prepare an ounce of two-part epoxy according to the manufacturer's directions. Lightly brush the resin onto the bottom of one paper pattern. Flip and place the paper atop the corresponding wing part, spanning the piece over the wire armature and making contact all around it. Repeat to affix the other three segments. Allow them to dry several hours or overnight (gravity will pull the paper down over the armature and fasten the epoxy to the wire).

6 Prepare another ounce of two-part epoxy. Flip the wings over (again keeping the component level) and apply tiny amounts of epoxy with a small brush or toothpick to the back. Allow the epoxy to pool a bit near the edges, reinforcing the juncture between the wire armature and the paper. Allow it to dry overnight.

7 Once dry, use a needle file or emery board to file the extra paper from the wings.

MATERIALS & TOOLS

■ STEEL WIRE,
   19 AND 28 GAUGE

■ JAPANESE CANDY PAPERS

■ TWO-PART EPOXY RESIN

■ TOOL KIT, PAGE 27

■ WAXED PAPER OR PLASTIC
   SHEET WORK SURFACE

■ SPONGE BRUSH,
   1 INCH (2.5 CM) WIDE

■ SMALL BRUSH
   OR TOOTHPICK

■ RING MANDREL

Completing the Ring

❶ Form the 2-inch (5.1 cm) wire tail into a spiral to make the head of the butterfly. Bend the head up slightly.

❷ Cut a 3-inch (7.6 cm) length of 28-gauge steel wire. Insert it through the center of the butterfly head and twist the two tails several times, into antennae shapes. Trim the ends to ¾ inch (1.9 cm). Using the tips of round-nose pliers, make tiny loops at the end of each antenna.

❸ Add a half size to the desired ring size.

❹ Straighten and wrap the remaining wire around the ring mandrel at the adjusted ring size three times (see drawing). Wrap the wire around the joint between the band and the butterfly several more times. Trim any remaining wire and tuck the end in to hide it.

❺ Cut a 36-inch (91.4 cm) length of 28-gauge wire. Wrap it around the three coils of the band close together, anchoring it under the butterfly at both ends. Cut the wire and hide the ends.

❻ Clean the wire portions of the butterfly ring, and seal them with wax.

Using funny words as often as possible gives me great joy. (I loved Dr. Seuss as a kid and wanted to insert myself, as Thing 3, right into the pages of *The Cat in the Hat*.) It's fun to say words like gobbledygook, bric-a-brac, and loosey goosey, and saying them out loud encourages laughter and a positive attitude. Give it a try! This Chunky Chockablock Tur-Kquoise Bracelet is as fun to say as it is to wear!

MATERIALS & TOOLS

■ **STEEL WIRE, 18 GAUGE OR THIN ENOUGH TO FIT SNUGLY THROUGH BEAD**

■ **8 BLOCK BEADS, VARIE-GATED TURQUOISE***

■ **TOOL KIT, PAGE 27**

■ **WHITE COLORED PENCIL OR SEAMSTRESS CHALK**

* MY HAND-DRILLED BEADS WOULD ONLY ACCOMMODATE 18-GAUGE WIRE, AND EVEN THEN, ONLY EIGHT BEADS OUT OF ALL OF THE BEADS FROM TWO STRANDS WOULD FIT THIS GAUGE.

CHUNKY CHOCKABLOCK TUR-KQUOISE

Forming the Bead Components

1 Cut eight pieces of steel wire, each 6 inches (15.2 cm) long.

2 Measure 2 inches (5.1 cm) from the end of one wire, and bend a right angle with flat-nose pliers. Repeat this step for the remaining seven wires.

3 Feed a bead onto one of the wires and snug it up to the bend. Using flat-nose pliers, grasp the wire on the other side of the bead and bend another right angle in the same direction as the first one.

4 Hammer the wire "legs" by moving the bead out of the way and pounding the free end. Repeat this step for all eight bead components.

Assembling the Bracelet

1 Lay out the beads in a pleasing order, with their wire "legs" pointed in the same direction.

2 Place the first two bead components next to each other with up to ¼ inch (6 mm) between them. Make pencil marks on the wire legs at the point where they meet the next bead. Bend a right angle back toward each leg, and trim the wire end to ⅜ inch (1 cm). Repeat process for all the wire legs.

3 Bend a plain loop at the end of each wire leg (drawing A). Connect the legs of the components by their loops, as shown in drawing B.

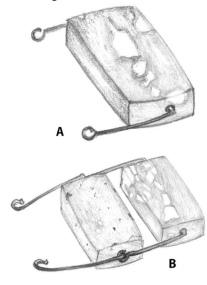

A

B

Forming the Closure

1 Check the bracelet's final size and mark the unattached pair of legs where the closure should be positioned.

2 Trim the wire leg ends ⅝ inch (1.6 cm) beyond the mark. Forge the wires and file their ends if needed.

3 With round-nose pliers, bend backward-facing curves at the points marked in step 2. Hook the curves onto the wires of the first component.

4 Clean the bracelet and finish it with wax.

My mother is the Queen of Homemade Pie Crust, but my pastry comes closer to the epoxy clay used in this mosaic cuff: hard as a rock and, well, let's just keep it at unappetizing. I thought it would be fun to crimp the edges of the cuff's focal area like Mom's pies. Following on this edible theme, the cuff's encrustations remind me of apples or cherries peeking through the tops of glistening turnovers. What a winning combination—jewelry that looks like dessert (except for the beetle crawling through). Mmmmm good!

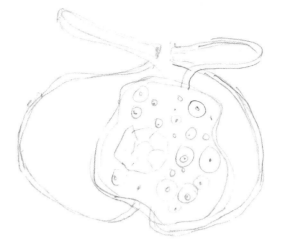

THE ROYAL ENCRUSTED CRUST

Forming the Cuff Armature

1 Cut a piece of 16-gauge steel wire, 24 inches (61 cm) long. Using the drawing on page 118 as a guide, form one-half of the wire armature. Start at the widest point of the template and work in the direction indicated. Flip the template 180 degrees and shape the other half of the armature. Cut the wire and file the ends.

2 Cut a piece of 28-gauge steel wire, 8 inches (20.3 cm) long. Bind the ends of the armature together. Hammer, clean, and seal the wire.

3 As shown in the drawing, gradually bend the wire armature around the mandrel. Keep your shaping consistent and even on both sides, and check the fit around your wrist often.

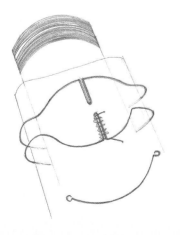

Adding the Encrusted Focal Piece

1 Following the manufacturer's instructions, mix the epoxy clay and hardener. Knead the two together until the color is consistent and the clay is soft and somewhat warm (2 to 3 minutes should do it). Roll two balls of clay, each about the size of a small egg.

2 One at a time, roll out the clay balls between two pieces of plastic wrap. Roll each ball into an imperfect circle that is at least ¼ inch (6 mm) larger than the circular center of the wire armature.

- STEEL WIRE, 16 AND 28 GAUGE
- METAL BEETLE OR OTHER STAMPING
- VARIOUS BEADS, SEQUINS, AND STEEL CUTS
- ACRYLIC PAINT IN BLACK, WHITE, GOLD, AND CRIMSON
- EPOXY CLAY
- TOOL KIT, PAGE 27
- MANDREL, 1⅝ INCHES (4.1 CM)
- PLASTIC FOOD WRAP
- SPONGE BRUSH, 1 INCH (2.5 CM) WIDE
- SPRAY FIXATIVE, MATTE OR SATIN

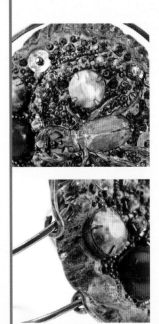

THE ROYAL ENCRUSTED CRUST

❸ Cover the mandrel with plastic wrap. Lay one clay circle on the mandrel, then place the wire armature on top of it. Place the second clay circle on top of the first, sandwiching the armature. (The mandrel helps the clay stay in a convex position on the armature as it dries). Lightly press the clay circles together and crimp both edges like pie dough.

❹ Embed the metal beetle or other stamping and the larger beads in the epoxy, then add the smaller sequins and beads. Press theses elements into the clay far enough so the clay slightly pops up over their edges. (Epoxy clay is not an adhesive, but it will harden around the embedded pieces, like a bezel.)

❺ Let the clay dry for an hour. Remove the bracelet from the mandrel and remove the plastic wrap. Allow the clay to finish drying overnight.

Embellishing the Cuff's Focal Area

❶ Cut two pieces of 16-gauge steel wire, each 4½ inches (11.4 cm) long. Form the wires to fit around the sides of the cuff's focal area and rest on top of it. Hammer and file the wires' ends.

❷ Bend a plain loop at one end of each wire. (You will use the loops to attach the wires to one side of the cuff.) Determine and mark where a second plain loop should be added so the wires can be attached to the other side of the cuff. Use round-nose pliers to bend a loop at the marked points.

❸ Seal the curved wires with wax. Use the loops to attach the wires to the cuff, just past the focal area.

Painting the Focal Area

❶ Make a wash of all of the acrylic paints, blending them with water to create a warm gray. Brush the color onto the hardened clay areas and let dry.

❷ Spray the fixative onto the dry painted clay. Let dry.

Three of my brother's boys play ice hockey. Their auntie prefers to see them on the bench or in the penalty box when they'd rather be out on the ice making slap-shot goals. Still, I can just see this pendant pressed up against one of their padded uniforms as they whoosh that puck toward the opposing team's goal ... getting shoved against the walls ... and checked, and elbowed, and hooked, ... and augh! It's more than this thin-skinned Auntie can take. Time out! (How 'bout a jewelry-making hobby instead?)

POWER PLAY

Preparing the Tin

1 Cut out the selected motif from the vintage tin. File the edges with needle files.

2 Measure and mark equidistant points around the perimeter of the motif, approximately every ¼ inch (6 mm). Using a center punch or awl, make a divot at each marked point.

3 Drill a ¹⁄₁₆-inch (1.6 mm) hole through each divot. Remove any burrs on the back of the tin with the larger drill bit, twisting it into the back of the hole by hand. Hammer the tin flat with a mallet.

Forming the Wire Frame

1 Cut a piece of 16-gauge steel wire, 12 inches (30.5 cm) long. Form the wire around a 2¾-inch (7 cm) mandrel and make a wrapped loop at the top. Hammer and clean the piece.

2 Measure and mark points around the wire at ¼-inch (6 mm) intervals. Use a file to carve a groove in the wire at each marked point.

Connecting the Tin to the Frame

1 Cut three or four 4-inch (10.2 cm) pieces of heavy thread and, as shown in the drawing, tie the tin piece to the frame to keep it in position.

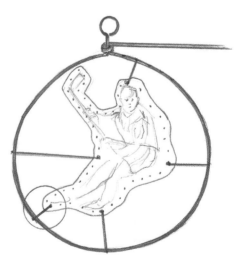

2 Cut 36 pieces of 24-gauge wire, varying the lengths from 3 to 5 inches (7.6 to 12.7 cm).

3 Bend a right angle ½ inch (1.3 cm) in from one wire end. Insert that end into a hole in the tin from the back, keeping the tin piece flat.

MATERIALS & TOOLS

- **STEEL WIRE, 16 AND 24 GAUGE**
- **VINTAGE TIN WITH DECORATIVE MOTIF**
- **WAXED IRISH LINEN OR ANY HEAVY THREAD**
- **TOOL KIT, PAGE 27**
- **DRILL BITS, 1/16 INCH (1.6 MM) AND 1/4 INCH (6 MM)**
- **AUTOMATIC CENTER PUNCH OR AWL**
- **NECKLACE FORM OR MANDREL**

4 Pull the wire toward the closest filed groove, go under and around the frame, and back to the upright wire tail. Tightly twist the wire around the upright tail three or four times without it buckling (see drawing). Tuck in the end with crimping pliers.

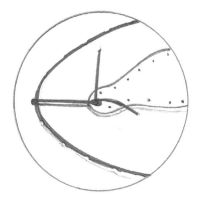

5 Trim the upright tail to 1/8-inch (3 mm) and tightly bend it down. Tuck it close to the knot with crimping pliers.

6 Select a key point on the opposite side of the tin piece and repeat steps 3 through 5.

7 Continue wrapping the wires, alternating sides, until the motif has been completely secured to the frame.

Forming the Neck Ring

1 Cut a piece of 16-gauge steel wire, 18 inches (45.7 cm) long. Use round-nose pliers to form a narrow U-shaped bend at the center of the wire. Measure 3/4 inch (1.9 cm) from the bottom of the U-shape. Bend a right angle on both sides of the U-shape at this point.

2 Work the remaining wire into a circle that is 6 inches (15.2 cm) in diameter, with the wire overlapping in the back. Use round-nose pliers to form a large plain loop in the wire at the point of intersection. Cut the other side of the wire, leaving enough length to form a hook. Use round-nose pliers to bend the hook and give it a jaunty angle.

3 Adjust the ring on a necklace form or mandrel so it hangs well.

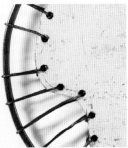

The pristine delicacy of lace can have a surprisingly dark quality. Its secrets run deep and its past is troubled. With only a flimsy alibi, this fragile flower was sentenced to repeated gluey douses and merciless drying on the rack. Oh, courageous Lace! What a proud and lovely martyr you've become!

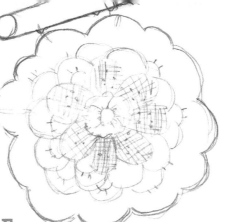

TORTURED LACE

MATERIALS & TOOLS

- STEEL WIRE, 16 GAUGE
- LACE, FLOWER PATTERNED
- IRISH WAXED LINEN, SLATE GRAY, 4 PLY
- TOOL KIT, PAGE 27
- PLASTIC BAG
- PVA GLUE
- DENATURED ALCOHOL
- WATER
- MANDREL, 1 INCH (2.5 CM)

Preparing the Lace Segment

1 Select and cut out a flower segment from the lace. Lay the flower segment flat on a plastic bag.

2 Mix 1 tablespoon of PVA glue, 1 tablespoon of water, and ½ tablespoon of denatured alcohol to make a stiffener solution. Liberally brush this solution onto the lace. Let dry. (The coated lace should be fairly rigid and plastic feeling. If needed, brush on additional layers of stiffener to achieve this result.)

Creating the Frame

1 Cut a piece of 16-gauge steel wire, 18 inches (45.7 cm) long. Bend small free-form curves in the wire, alternately using large round-nose pliers and flat-nose pliers.

2 Bend a plain loop in each wire end. Connect the loops to close the wire form. Hammer and clean the wire form, then seal it with wax.

Attaching the Lace

1 Cut four pieces of the waxed linen, each 4 inches (10.2 cm) long. Separate the plies into 16 separate threads.

2 Center the lace in the wire frame. As shown in the top right drawing, tie each petal to the wire with a knot. Trim the threads to ³⁄₁₆ inch (5 mm).

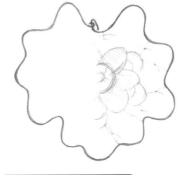

Forming the Fibula

1 Cut a piece of 16-gauge steel wire, 8 inches (20.3 cm) long. Using the drawing below as a template, bend the wire into the fibula design.

2 Use round-nose pliers to bend the double-back end over the pin, forming the catch. File the end of the pin to a sharp point.

3 Lay the bottom portion of the fibula against a 1-inch (2.5 cm) mandrel. Use two pairs of flat-nose pliers to bend sharper angles to within ¼ inch (6 mm) of each end. Slip the fibula into the top of the frame.

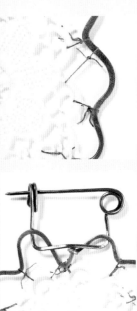

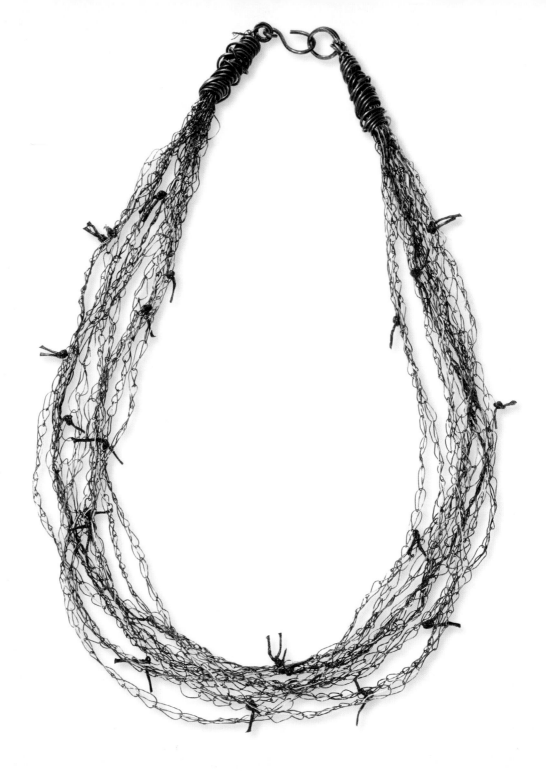

I n a perfect world, cows would know to stay in their own pastures and not be runnin' willy nilly about the countryside. Alas, they are cows and need a little more "encouragement" to stay on the side of the fence where the grass is-what-it-is. Perhaps a cow/farmer compromise is in order——one where Bossie negotiates with Farmer Brown to borrow this kinder-gentler, soft-barbed fence "technology." Just a thought.

COMFY COZY BARBED WIRE

Crocheting the Chains

① Working directly off the 28-gauge coil, make 10 chain-stitched lengths of wire crochet, each 20 inches (50.8 cm) long with 2- to 3-inch (5.1 to 7.6 cm) tails at both ends. Don't start the crochet with a slipknot, as you would with yarn; instead, start with a small twisted loop. You may need to tug on the wire to keep the loops all the same size. If the loop is too big, ease some of the wire back out.

② Clean the crocheted wire chains, and seal them with wax.

Decorating the Chains

① Cut 10 different-colored pieces of the 4-ply thread, each 20 inches (50.8 cm) long. Separate the plies, and set aside three of them for another project.

② Thread a large-eyed needle with one of the plies and weave it back and forth through every other stitch in one wire crochet chain. Double-knot the thread end to the last wire loop. Trim the thread closely. Apply adhesive to the knotted thread, and let it dry overnight. Repeat this step for all the chains, using a different color thread for each one.

③ Cut 20 pieces of the 7-ply thread, each 2 inches (5.1 cm) long. Use a double knot to tie the threads around the crocheted wire chains at pleasing intervals. Trim the tails of the knots to ⅜ inch (1 cm).

④ Lay the wire chains parallel to each other, and line up their ends evenly.

Forming the Cones & Clasp

① Cut two pieces of 19-gauge steel wire, each 24 inches (61 cm) long.

② Hold all 10 chains together in a bundle. Insert one of the 19-gauge wires into a crocheted loop approximately 1 inch (2.5 cm) from one end of the bundle.

③ Wrap the wire around the bundle of crocheted chains, tightly and a bit haphazardly, into a cone shape. Trim the starting end of the wrap to ⅜ inch (1 cm), and tuck it inside the cone. Use round-nose pliers to make a triple loop in the other end of the wrapped wire cone.

④ Repeat steps 2 and 3 on the other end of the crocheted chain bundle.

⑤ Cut two pieces of 16-gauge steel wire, each 2 inches (5.1 cm) long. Form one of the wires into a small S-hook. Form the other wire into a jump ring with a ⅝-inch (8 mm) inner diameter. Trim the excess wire. Hammer the hook and the jump ring.

⑥ As shown in the drawing, attach the clasp halves to the triple loops at the end of the necklace. Clean the cones and the clasp, and seal them with wax.

- STEEL WIRE, 28 GAUGE, ON COIL
- STEEL WIRE, 16 AND 19 GAUGE
- WAXED IRISH LINEN THREAD, 4 PLY, 10 COLORS
- WAXED IRISH LINEN THREAD, 7 PLY, BLACK
- TOOL KIT, PAGE 27
- CROCHET HOOK, SIZE G (4 MM)
- NEEDLE WITH LARGE EYE
- WATCHMAKER'S GLUE
- MANDREL, ⁵⁄₁₆ INCH (8 MM)

DEDICATION

For My Three Boys:

To my colorblind and very traditional husband, Mr. Black-and-White. You could have married practically and sensibly, but instead, you chose me! You found success (my Midas Man) by learning your way around the challenges of dyslexia (there is no stronger problem solver). You're a generous and loving father, friend, brother, and son. You're an inspiration and the love of my whole live-long life!

To James, whose dry wit and wry sense of humor make me forget you're not an adult yet. I love you like Moms love their first-borns—with super-sized ecstasy and fear!

To Liam, my fine-featured kiddo! May the glint in your eye always mean there's a new idea and some ingenious project brewing just beneath the surface. I love you ad infinitum!

ACKNOWLEDGMENTS

For kicking this one off: Mary Wohlgemuth and side-kicks (in this case) Karin Buckingham and KPC Books.

For beginning the thing: Mindy Brooks, Sandi Keiser, Naomi Fujimoto, Linda Augsburg, Cathy Jakicic, and Jane Konkel.

For lifting and nudging: Marlene Vail, Linda Kollatz, Joel Wingelman, and Kristen Jastroch.

For picking it up: Marthe Le Van (who saw something in my work that ended up being a little book about steel wire—thank you!). You are amazing on so many levels.

For dusting it off: Gavin Young (for her patience, cheer-leading, quick response, kindness, and calm throughout this whole process).

For shaking it out: Kristi Pfeffer, Steve Mann, Kathy Holmes, Carol Barnao, and everyone else (who mixed, melded, and molded these words and pictures into a bee-you-tee-full book!).

For tweaking and 'splaining: Patrice Lantier (my friend, ex-boss, and now writing coach, the best ever!).

For upping the ante: All the wonderful artists who have graced this book's gallery and have lent the inspiration of their work.

For propping me up: Jill Erickson and the *Art Jewelry* crew (it's Hamma'-time!).

For setting the scene: Karen Bolton, Serials Librarian, Walter Schroeder Library at Milwaukee School of Engineering.

For pretty-ing the picture: Deone Jahnke, Steve Mann, and Tom Fritz (not your ordinary photogs)!

For sharing the love: Keith Lo Bue, Susan Lenart Kazmer, Robert Dancik, Charles Lewton-Brain, Michael deMeng, Arline Fisch, and the Queen of Quiet Exuberance, Sr. Mary Rosemarita Huebner.

For pounding and polishing: Rebecca Conrad-LaMere, studio assistant and friend whose happy presence in my studio makes it look like I'm not always laughing and talking to myself! And to Kat Feldman, the "New Gal!"

For putting up: All my friends and family, for understanding my obsession and livin' it with me.

For joining the trip: My LBSers—one and all! Hello!

For being my water-cooler community: each and every Facebook friend!

For teaching the teacher: My students, former and future, who stir the maker in me every day I stand before them.

Brenda Schweder has good-naturedly embraced many labels in her lifetime, from A Little Bit Steampunk to a Little Bit Tree Hugger to The Little Red-Haired Girl (back when *A Charlie Brown Christmas* still captured the attention of all good little boys and girls). Her latest monikers are Bend-it Like Brenda and Iron woMan (thanks to her friends Jill and Jill, for helping her realize her left arm is now growing larger than her right), due to her most unfeminine passion for creating jewelry with steel wire (grrrrr!).

Schweder's designs and fashion jewelry forecasts have been published over 100 times in books and magazines, including: *30-Minute Earrings* (Lark Crafts, 2010), *30-Minute Necklaces* (Lark Crafts, 2010), *Art Jewelry*, *Bead Style*, *Bead &*

Button, *BUST*, *Vintage Style Jewelry*, *Make it Mine*, *Wirework 2010*, *Crystal Chic*, and many other compilations, pamphlets, and books. In addition to *Steel Wire Jewelry*, Schweder is the author of *Junk to Jewelry* and *Vintage Redux*.

Schweder has hit the online community via Alison Lee of www.craftcast.com, where she's taught and been featured in an online podcast interview. Her Tweedy Turquoise Brooch was recreated in an episode of *Beads, Baubles & Jewels* (PBS).

Also a nationally-recognized teacher and jewelry designer, Schweder is an instructor at Mount Mary College and offers workshops at beading venues such as The Bead & Button Show (Milwaukee, Wisconsin) and others coast to coast.

Contact her via e-mail at b@brendaschweder.com, visit her website at www.brendaschweder.com, catch her on Facebook, and read her blog at www.brendaschweder.blogspot.com.

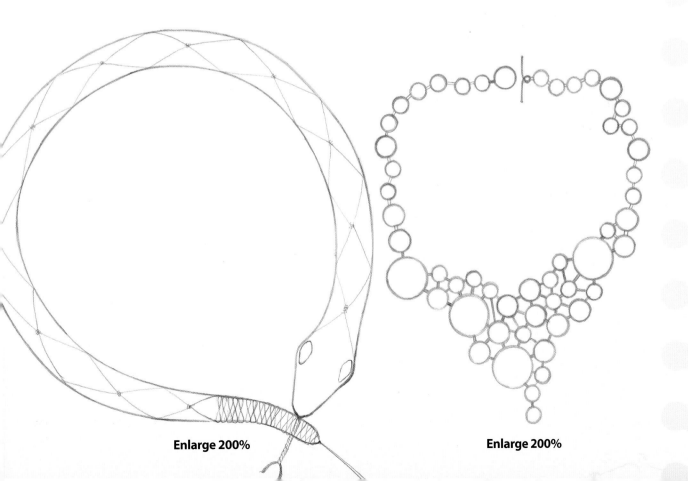

Enlarge 200%　　　　　**Enlarge 200%**

INDEX

GALLERY ARTIST INDEX

It's all on www.larkcrafts.com

Daily blog posts featuring needlearts, jewelry and beading, and all things crafty

Free, downloadable **projects** and **how-to videos**

Calls for artists and **book submissions**

A free **e-newsletter** announcing new and exciting books

...and a place to celebrate the **creative spirit**